ESSAYS ON
ART EDUCATION
IN INDIA
AND OTHERS

I0479923

BABU NAMBOODIRI K

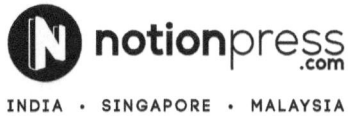

INDIA · SINGAPORE · MALAYSIA

Notion Press

No. 8, 3rd Cross Street,
CIT Colony, Mylapore,
Chennai, Tamil Nadu - 600 004

First Published by Notion Press 2020
Copyright © Babu Namboodiri K 2020
All Rights Reserved.

ISBN 978-1-64919-970-6

Dedicated

To my Teacher

Japanese Artist "Kinutani Kouji"

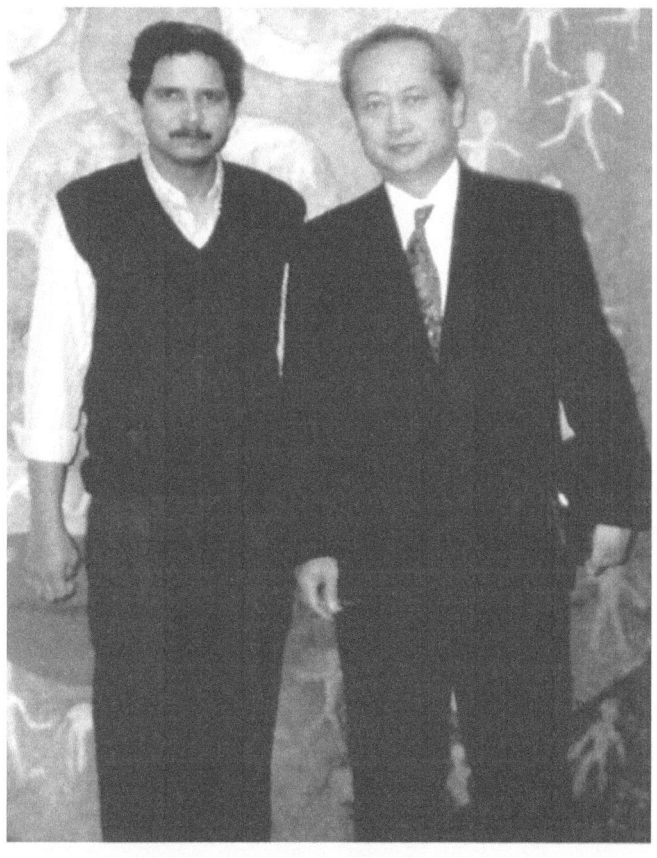

Babu Namboodiri K with Kinutani Kouji. Tokyo. 2000.

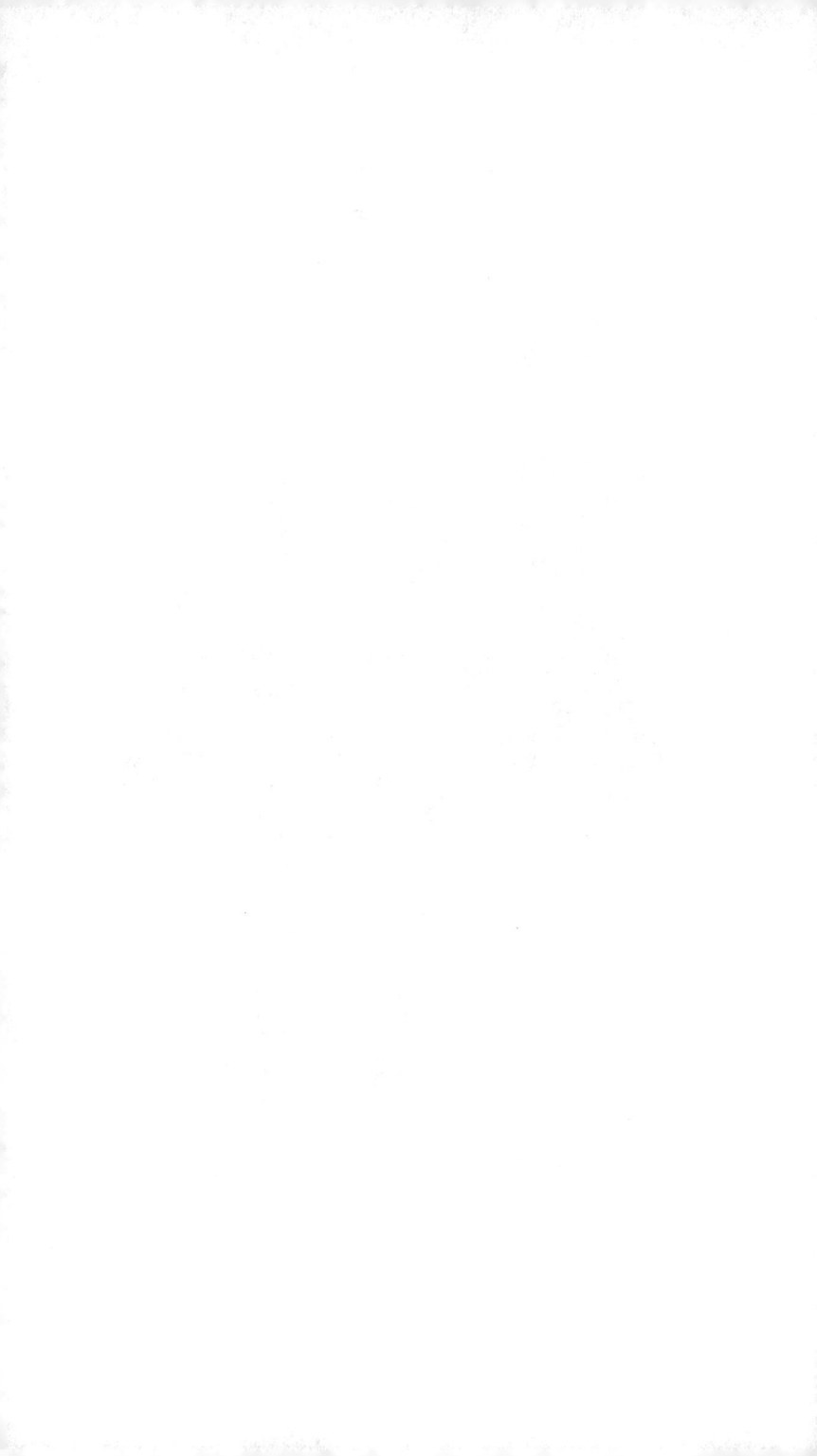

*My sincere gratitude to everyone
who helped and supported writing this book and
publishing.*

Contents

Foreword

The term Art Education is commonly used to mean the process of training in Visual art which includes painting, Sculpture, the Graphic arts etc. In the present day context education in these arts includes their theory, history, Practice and techniques of production. In the past, any object produced skillfully and aesthetically was seen as art. They were seen also as products of creative imagination. Later in the twentieth century, the introduction of theoretical studies in the curriculum of courses in art lead art objects gaining much more meaningful presence.

Writings by the artists, art teachers and critics have contributed greatly to moulding and nurturing the field of art education in India. We gratefully acknowledge the contributions of E B Havell, Ananda K Coomaraswamy, Abanindranath Tagore, Rabindranath Tagore, Mulk Raj Anand, K G Subramanyan and many other visionaries for what they have done through their writings to Indian Art. It is a challenging task for an experienced teacher to take up such a venture of research into record his observations and present in the form of a book. Here is a book titled "Essays on Art Education In India and Others" by Babu Namboodiri K, the text of which has been shown from the researches he has carried.

In these essays (chapters 1-7) the author takes us back to the period when the 'guide' system or apprentice ship was on practice. Later tracing various courses of art production he comes to the nineteenth century India, the period which saw establishing art schools in major cities like Madras, Bombay, Calcutta, Patna and Trivandrum during colonial period by the British and provincial kingdoms. He essays at length about the political as well as social situations which formed the backdrop for the founding of these training centers in art and crafts. Mr. Babu also delves into various anecdotes pertaining to the up gradation of the curriculum and the status of the institution in the social context. The essays also throw light on various academic and administerial aspects associated with the establishments of art institutions later in the country.

Babu Namboodiri K has also appended three chapters (others), in chapters 8 and nine he gives an account of the indigenous craft traditions and ritual art forms of Kerala while the 10th chapter is a documented work on leather puppetry. These essays have been written after exquisite documentation and research carried out. The author has shown great insight into interpreting the indigenous ritual, performing art form and craft traditions through his lucid writing. I hope this book will be well rec eived by the readers.

– **K C Chitrabhanu**

20.07.20   **Trivandrum.**

Introduction

The essays written and published by me in different occasions on various publications including International digital Journals are included in this book. As Art and Art Education are my major work and professional area, it is but natural that the elaboration of subject matter focuses on "Art Education" is quiet ordinary. Even the terms Art, Art Education and Literary activities for publishing have contradictory nature and outcomes of creative elements; it can be justified only because of its innovative nature and progressive outlook.

I think it is essential to discuss the situation which made me aware of the relevance of such writing. The writings based on factual incidents, space and time are the relevant factors when describing an incident in the view of making it a historical action. Also the background of the writer, the writers wisdom on the particular issue describing and the ability of writer to narrate the incidents and occasions in relation with space and time where then incidents' it took place, his psychological attitude towards the happenings in his surroundings most of the time without own involvement are certain elements of relevance here. Even though the historical happenings are of unique characteristics, and its nature of existing with similar altitude unchangingly forever, the sincere studious activities towards its objectiveness can establish the real time facts to even to the forth coming generations ever after Centuries. The depth of the facts drilled out can rebuild the factuality to the current static world. It is an unchanging reality.

Even though changing of direction according to the narrators ability is an ordinary unexplainable phenomenon, several times the change in direction of the narration taking a far away distance from the real objectivity is humanitarian. Due to the amount of power utilized in changing the direction in measures of higher altitudes, the work out of phenomenal change reshapes the objectivity of historical incident. The beings who follow such documentation shall not be communicated but mislead. In that case when the narration with theatrical effects is powerful than real incident exposures, the factual history will not exists and the false documentation will sustain. The dramatically described story shall take attention of human and factual historical process will lose its faces.

When we engage on deep studies with curiosity and special inborn interest towards Art, the studious beings get a clear idea of the differences between factual incidences and documented evidences of incidents. These kinds of arrivals at falsely fabricated ideas in the historical scenarios, make loss of believability on documentations is said to be factual incidents. The process of historical development has attracted me because it is propagated to maintain time, space objectivity bound relations towards various objectivities. These are some of the factors that directed and confirmed my arrival at these kinds of creative destinations.

I was deeply interested in painting since birth opted to choose it as life's vocation, reached College of Fine arts, Trivandrum after normal college studies. I began and seek art historical studies as a part of practical art studies during my course. I have understood that such kind of studies have relevance when art practice is widely concerned. The interest in historical and aesthetical revelations in art led me to the theoretical studies on art along with practical art practice after studies on Practical painting in post graduate level at the College of Art New Delhi in early 1990s. My masters including Prof. C L Porinchukutty, Late Professors K V Haridas, Om Prakash Sharma and K S Kulkarni have appreciated me for my success in practical career as an artist and for the enthusiasm towards theoretical studies. It was my personal interest that took me to engage on research activities with the guidance of well-known Indian novelist and Cultural activist Mulk Raj Anand. This turn of accepting theoretical studies was due to inspirations from the then Ambassador for Netherlands in India, an art lover and art collector Mrs. Egjie M Schoo and well-known Museum practitioners Dr. L P Sihare and Dr. Anis Faroqui. Those studies led me to the International Research studies on Practical painting at The Tokyo National University of Fine Arts (Geidai) with Mombusho fellowship in late 1990s.

The attitude that has developed during research studies in India and abroad surely helped me to continue my studious activities to a greater extend. As my area of work and studies are practical painting and due to my special interest in painting I kept both kinds of activities along with my day to day life ahead. I have continued my aggressive initiatives to carry research activities along with professional Practical painting, and still I hold on to the same. Also I tried to keep my studious activities bound with enquiries on the maintenance of ideological relations with accurate evidences for historical existence. But I am also depended on similar objectivities and happenings for accurate historical data formulation of the history in the making.

This is a collection of essays published by me during various occasions and well appreciated by its readers. I thought bringing these essays together under one title can result the readers a safe and intact feeling among readers, which provide more solid understanding towards the factors discussed elaborately in its chapters. These are coordinated facts of matters which prove historical nature. I tried to develop a coordinated feeling of factual entities elaborately discussed in the chapters of this book. It is not just discussion (for discussion) but factual issues and happenings took shape during past several centuries, the incidents left deep marks in the pages of time which is not over the skin of the social animal but rooted deep inside the blood vessels gushing to heart of the systems.

First of all I would like to point out that it was not accidental for me to choose the topic Art Education for writing these essays. As I am an artist is engaged in professional work and is continuously teaching art, it was impossible for me to avoid think about Art Education in a very lively manner. When I was eager to know how art teaching system has evolved in to its present form, I went through a ready search for written matter but it was very disappointing to know there was no such readily available booked knowledge. I had to search for data, assemble them, study and assimilate them in to shape through with the reasons of several happenings and assess them with my limited knowledge and evaluate with accessed awareness. In the past several years Art Education took several changes. Art education was not lonely phenomena took shape in a corner of a village but an individual growth of a surviving mechanism based on cultural changes in a prolonging manner took shape into exhilaration. In this introduction I shall try to brief the matters which I have seriously evaluated for understanding the nature of changes posed in the last centuries all over the globe to the current day situation.

In the first essay I am trying to evaluate the nature and characteristics of Modernization, in its ongoing development and the changes happened to its meaning in the human minds. Modernization of Art takes place when an artist with great imagination involves in creation through experimentation. The existing values which have been accepted for the past several decades are experimented and evaluated again and again during the new process of modernization. Modernization has unique characteristics based on the objectivity to which it is targeted. There was no Art School that a talented person could attend until the Thirteenth Century, when formal teaching method to teach art was formulated. Modernization of art education is a result of sensitive processes that took shape with influences of society from where it took formation which caused for its survival.

In the second essay I have elaborately explained about status of the country, India as a Sensitive Background for

Art Education. "It was fundamental for the diverse cultural institutions in India which managed establishments of education to the society in the course of its constant existence even if this relation restricted all resources of fortitude for its subsistence, due to various factors, but religious reasons were at prime. They continued teaching until they got vanished from the history. Hinduism, Buddhism, Brahmanism and Jainism are major among them and each of them introduced unique art education systems through ideological expansion and their own survival. It was followed by the Mughal Empire who encouraged Miniature Painting and Company School came into survival on prolongation of this which supported materialization of art activities to appeal Western sensibilities. Ravi Varma was totally criticized for his manifestations with oil painting: a Western device but Bengal school proved its name for being more Indian through their propaganda. The school established by Rabindranath Tagore at Santiniketan was an answer for many questions: the new beginnings from here and with emergence of individual activities by various geniuses, a style accepted by international appreciators began to stage in India and which lead to new developments in Art Education.

In the essay titled "Modernization in art education as measured with ancient parameters to current" I have discussed about the growth of Indian atmosphere of Art education to an advanced level of art implementing state. It is a traditional approach to teach art students by engaging an art teacher himself in production of art works for a certain period. That enables the student to create art with only own efforts and made absolutely able him forever for the same. Through on several centuries various religions held its own role in teaching art to a student while mandatorily sticking on to its own values. Each religious commune was competing with the other to acquire their own style of teaching art since art was socially accepted as a means of ideological communication, which is transparent for any onlooker. Florentine school of Italy is an outstanding example for creating absolutely talented creative artists and theoreticians like Michelangelo, Raphael, Giorgio Vasari and so on. The existence of art activities and its establishment made a kind of 'public art teaching' around the globe.

The society began to accept certain parameters established by artists in its hinterland. The society understood to evaluate art of each period with scales developed within that period. The Royal Art society of England and Salon de Art, Paris were two institutions where activities existed in connection with historical importance in the end of 19th century. The exhibition organized by rejected artists of Salon de Paris in 1863 with the help of Napolean III got popularized in the globe as 'Salon de Refuses' and that created extremely new scaling parameters in the society. The Bauhaus School with the ideologies of Walter Gropius, Moholy Nagy and Paul Klee, challenged all the prevailing styles in teaching art and established a new one. Centered at various cities in Germany, Bauhaus school initiated new teaching methods. But the anti-human approaches during Second World War stopped this initiative for the time being. Many Bauhaus school artists suffered at the hands of Nazi activists. With the advent of Hitler, Bauhaus school genius scattered all over the world. The artists of Bauhaus school spread all over the world and maintained a standard of its own by entering into social lives of the venues where ever they are in.

Various critical factors which required care for the maintenance of Modernization on Art education in India are evaluated in the next essay. Modernization process that took place on Art Education in India was a continuation of similar processes that took place in various venues all over the world, beginning from the Florentine School which supported many major artists like Michelangelo. There is a straight clear path definable from 15 century developments and through Salon de Refuses in Paris, and establishments of various schools all over the World to the modern developments in India. In India British promoted art production in the lines of their tastes- they educated Indian Artists to produce art to match their tastes. In the past there were several developments which promoted an art education system which had roots with Bauhaus school of Europe. Starting from the initiation of Kalabhavana by Tagore, also we brought it in to the line of progress. It requires special care to keep the attitude of modernization while evaluating all different affecting vibrations including changes in our walks of lives.

The special role of E B Havell on manifestation of Indian ideals in art education is discussed in the following essay. Due to the attitudes of its officials and British Colony rule the art education in India and art practice by the beneficiaries were facing various problems of identity and originality. Many art schools began to function with the inspirations received from the great exhibition of 1851 with initiatives of private individuals and collaborations for the enhancement of art activities in India but could not take any solid action towards improvement of the prevailing situations. E B Havell, a British art official took initiatives to change the situations responsibly and challengingly with the help of Indian art enthusiasts. The career of E B Havell was cut short from British part, said to be due to mental breakdown and never returned to India after 1908. But the introductions of Indian ideals continued vigorously by his Indian friends following his objectivities.

Ernest Binfield Havell (16 September 1861 – 31 December 1934), who was well known in the name E.B. Havell, was a powerful Art administrator and Art Historian. He was in India for more than two decades in connection with the progress of Art Education. He was the author of several books on Indian art and architecture. Being a member to Havell family of artists and art educators, he was the appointed principal of the Government School of Art, Calcutta from 1896 to 1905. With the companionship of artists in Tagore Family, especially with Abanindranath Tagore, he managed to develop a style of art and art education based on Indian ideals rather than the then established Western models, which led to the foundation of the Bengal school of art. Here this study focuses on the various elements that supported him, evaluates the kind of modernism he could insist in art education and art practice, how he maintained the various relevant situations and tackled his involvement in a manner that logically fits onto a passionate Art Enthusiast.

The family background of Tagore was economically and culturally stable enough to accommodate and manage any sort of social situations. Rabindranath was surrounded by a crowd of people with immense of creative energy and he was largely introduced and appreciated for creative pursuits in literature. He was grown with the feeling that he was not capable enough to make expressions through visual art creations and has enviously witnessed the nephews challengingly involving in visual creative pursuits and getting widely appreciated. The art education system in India those days were meant only to support privileges of a British colony. A group of people thoughtfully and vigorously made initiatives but they could only make marginal differences in the ongoing situations under British power. With great ideals Rabindranath Tagore began to establish Santiniketan since 1921 as a university. He came in contact with the modern Western Art education and self realized his capabilities to express through visual art creations and practiced western basics for his expression. Also he established modern art education system with necessary additions of Indian basics in Santiniketan with the help of geniuses in house.

Rabindranath was born as the fourteenth child to Debendranath (son of Dwarakanath Tagore) within the Tagore clan in 1861. Rabindranath held a lonely childhood due to his busy parents and was grown up in the charge of servants. Being the brother of thirteen elders in the family, apart from his father Rabindranath had strong influence of his elder brothers. Among the elder brothers, Jyothirindranath, (the fifth son of Devendranath) and his wife Kadambari devi and had an affectionate relation to Rabindranath. Kadambari Devi had attraction towards literary pursuits, appreciated largely the literary pursuits of Rabindranath from very beginning. While Jyothiridranath played the guardianship of Rabindranath meticulously Kadambaridevi supplied the emotional stimulus, caressing warmth and shade all of which supported the growth of novel personality of Rabindranath to a creative genius.

The two chapters followed by the above discussion are focusing on another relevant issue with on craft production in Kerala. The first one is about social set up prevailed in India which caused craft production. It is titled as Societal Situations underneath Craft Ethnicity in Kerala. Kerala is situated in the far south of India facing the Arabian Sea and shares its boundaries with Karnataka and Tamil Nadu. There are several craft forms prevalent in Kerala which receives pampering from unique social situations persisting there. These craft activities are shaped with acceptance of current social circumstances prevailing there as a continuation of societal activity formations from the past. These productions are results of persisting demands from the society for the sake of such objectivities. Scenario of social life forms the platform for active participation of these objectivities in humanitarian spaces. Such demands are forwarded through special roles of typical objectivities in social life practices and through social life. This special active role is generated through habits of the society with its own social limitations, like behavioral attitudes, habitual practices, availability of natural rescores, and explorations like economical situations, philosophical awareness, devotional practice, and psychological ambience or religious participatory activities. Each time these craft forms took form of life even without acknowledgement of social plants with which they are attached but justified on social relevance and absolute necessity of getting it shaped as it is.

The essay titled A Variety of Ethnicities on Craft Conception Habituated in Premises of Kerala Describes about the caste system which supported craft production in Kerala. There are a number of conformist skill based forms extensively prevalent in instantaneous circumstances which are clearly visible for ordinary human beings. As a matter of fact, these innovative forms are part of an average power of human survival and performances of these social mechanisms are unavoidable for its existence. Many mechanisms are invented for reducing difficulties of employment and with the use of them strains are evacuated to negligible. Apart from useful aspects common men like them to contain a shape that enhances the aesthetic sensibilities of its beholder. On anticipation of this specific utility these mechanisms are well planned before creation. There are several activities that come under ones purview when us seriously looked upon for its significance. In this study several venues of craft production are elaborately explained and its social relevance on materialistic and an Aesthetic utility are pointed out. The craft productions found in Kerala has two phases, the first one is with excess of labor content in it and other is with more aesthetic or philosophic content. Necessity of further studies in this area is exposed and confirmed.

With stupendous international kindred, leather shadow puppetry is a marvelous folk art form widespread in India. This art form has a role in conception of amusement in all south Indian states, (Kerala, Tamil Nadu, Karnataka and Andhra Pradesh). Apart from its special role on Hindu devotional practices it a well established engagement of entertainment. There are certain families absolutely devoted in puppet making, playing and surviving only with income produced through performances. It is very intricate for provide a normal survival to them because of the strong hostility with other various modern forms of entertainments existing in each corner. However it is the duty of the beholders and beneficiaries to keep the system alive for their continued existence. The certain changes and differences found in puppets and its manipulation in Andhra Pradesh are documented and evaluated its relevance here.

I hope that this book shall be informative and mind refreshing experience to its readers.

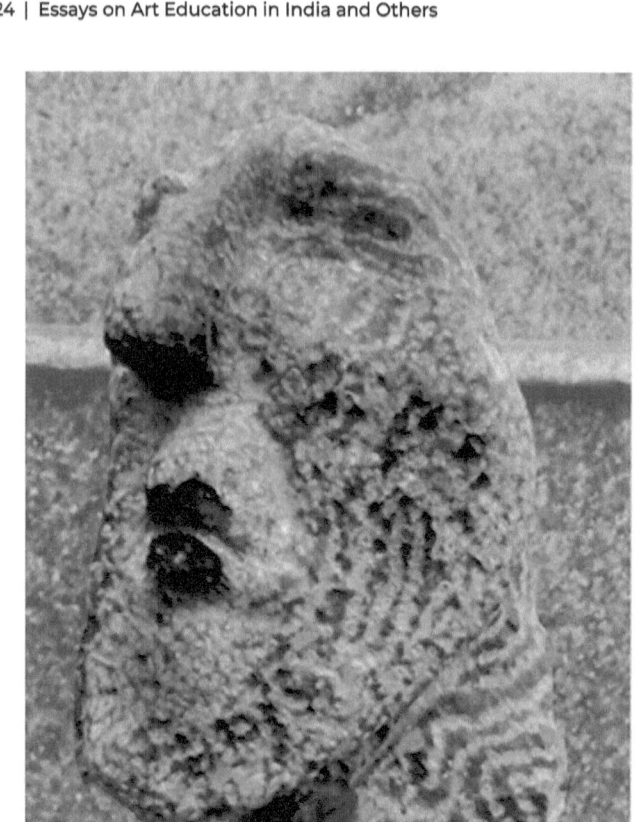

**Transformation of image into 3 dimensional accidental forms;
Sculpture by C. Dakshinamurti, 1996, 10 inches x 6inches x 6 inches.**

CHAPTER
02

The Nature and Characteristics of Modernization in Art

Abstract: Modernization of Art takes place when an artist with great imagination involves in creation through experimentation. The existing values which have been accepted for the past several decades are experimented and evaluated again and again during the new process for modernization. Modernization has unique characteristics based on the objective to which it is targeted. There was no art school that a talented person could attend until the Thirteenth Century, when a formal teaching method to teach art was formulated. Modernization of Art Education is a result of sensitive processes that took shape with the influences of society from where it took form for its survival.

Key Words: Modernization, Comparison, Experiment, Research, Society, Creativity, Artist, Teaching, Imagination, Aesthetics.

Modernization[1] of Art happens when an artist with great imagination[2] involves in creation through experimentation[4].

The nature of his experimentations depends upon the audacity and capability of the artist to express his feelings towards his own surroundings. The experimentation begins with comparison of various potentials against outstanding credentials of the current incident. Scaling the difference in materialistic and idealistic qualities between two values and its acceptance by the public defines the very word 'Comparison'[2]. The existing values which have been accepted for the past several decades are experimented and evaluated again and again during the processes for modernization.

The words 'Research'[3] and 'Experiment'[4] are by and largely used to indicate and elucidate the recent scientific developments in our immediate surroundings. It is not fair if this matter is not rethought just because there are several critics who point out that usage of the words 'Research' and 'Experimentation' are inappropriate due to various reasons. Process of Research and Experimentation are viewed as an open door for emancipation of thought process since an expounding studious practice has the ability to access creativity in art if the author is equipped with necessary communication skills. The ways for acquiring the potential for each work is entirely different from one another. The continuous flow of currents through the established path ways leads us to the special target.

The scientific researches and experiments aim at developments in the related fields only. Aesthetic[10] sensibilities lead to the materialistic and ideological growth of human generations. The aim of art has always been to produce aesthetics. The aesthetic sense is transformative in nature and it adapts to the various changes in its environment. The artist, being a social monster, cannot stop himself from adapting manners according to the reflected manners of the environment. Certain examples are mentioned here to highlight that the work (labor) of artist is highly reformative. The modernization of any objectivity is possible only when the creators agree to unfasten their attitudes towards various creative approaches and related studious activities, against the recommended state of affairs. This factor will be crystal clear to a receptor of open mind, if he is ready to examine the existential substances of any human race including the current. Let us now covenant with some related factors here.

In the past century a scientist who was busy with scientific experiments, built a railway track in order to bring loose soil from various corners of the country to the premises of his residence. Soon the premise of the house was filled with tones of the similar raw material (loose soil) from various parts of the country, and this continued for decades. It was not easy to conduct suitable physical and chemical experiments in each molecule of the soil content; however he created a system of thorough filtration and careful examination, and stored them in specifically labeled test tubes. With the initiation of highly creative, specially considered, uniquely planned programs, the experimentation continued for several decades without impediment.

At last, the scientist located the rootlet of a radioactive element for the first time in the universe. The scientists were on continuous research for several years to find an element which could emit radiation. This was the peculiar and fastidious methodology for modernization in scientific fields. Such activity establishes the tediousness in the process of modernization. At the same time this indicates the importance of the gathering sufficient knowledge to modify personal lives aiming at the social concern. Since the evaluation focuses on the magnitude and mannerisms of entirely different parameters that exists in all objects and objectivities of human existence, (like areas of Science, History, Language, Visual language etc.), the spectators are permitted to engage in analysis to understand the depth of all engagements the creator dwells in. The relevance and ambience of the final product depends upon the nature of the unfiltered raw materials in the beginning. The nature of raw materials controls the characteristics of the required experiments to produce a meaningful object from it and the relevance of the object is the result of experimentation.

Another important factor that influences modernization is imagination[7]. It is an accepted fact that only a psychological situation enriched by useful wisdom will support the advent of modernization. It requires discoursing and analyzing another scientific fact to acknowledge the phenomenal role of imagination in modernization. It has been criticized by several aestheticians for its materialistic approach but it counter argued with a fact that beauty cannot be visualized when certain a level involvement of materials are absent in the representation of realities. Representations cannot be activated without utilizing the basic nature of matter through the various forms of power.

Each element in the universe is unique, and reacts with other similar elements, based on duration of contact with the other, various surrounding situations; and the distance of placement between each other. These properties are rare and often subjected to change with effects of its surroundings. A scientist arranged all the elements which were then known in the world in a table according to their individual properties and their nature of reaction with the other elements. With the identification and acknowledgement of atomic number, the scientist included all known elements in the universe in the list in a peculiar order. Having done this, it was noticed that there were some empty spaces in the table when the atomic number was followed. It was concluded that several elements were missing from the table and were yet to be discovered. Based on this conclusion, in the future, scientists regularly went on experiments and were able to identify some new elements in universe, thereby filling the gaps in the table and developing the periodic table as we see it today in connection with atomic number.

True imagination works in this direction. The imagination should begin from the existing truths, and then only they can be completely original and relevant to the existing world. This fact is completely transparent in creative art production. Only the imagination centered on the basically existing creative visual realities can succeed getting live feel of existence in creative pursuits successfully. Creativity[8] is the next word that requires an explanation here, in this connection. Creativity is considered here as the ability of the creator to involve in aesthetic production though creation. It is deeply rooted in the basic foundations of the productive clan that the artist survives and belongs to. Even if the existence is marginal the notion of survival spreads over the egos of the society. The society embarks upon the logic of its existence in general with genuine ideological friction. As a product of all of the above, the creator works on essential substance in his limit, he experiments and physically engages in creation by using his individual talent of creativity. So that the beauty of the aesthetic object he creates is strictly a product of an established and specifically formulated characteristics of the society in which he lives in. The artist experiences the society around him and creates an art work in a form that is suitable to carry his feelings to the viewer. Here the viewer is not just single person but all as a whole.

Modernization[1] always happened by emancipation of the abilities acquired by the creator during friction with their own contemporary factors. In the platform provided by the society, each artist is actively engaging in enquiry on possibilities of self modernization and a creative process for self expression simultaneously. The artist analyses the existing aesthetic sensibilities and creates a form by experiment, action to replace all the existing and prevailing aesthetic sensibilities with new ones of higher value. He makes it possible by harsh communications with the surroundings. By this process, practiced over centuries, modernization was imbibed to art gradually. The characteristics of Modern society provoke all the creative efforts and make pathways for expressions of advanced emotions through phenomenal changes named "isms".

Teaching is equal to learning. It is not two but three phenomena. 'Teaching'[9] is the first activity. During the 'teaching' process, the teacher tries to develop a communicative language with the students and the teacher learns to communicate in a visual language produced by him. The student learns while teaching is conducted. In the case of visual arts, the teacher is developing an efficient visual language purely based on Aesthetics[10]. These simple teaching methodologies began in traditional setups. As a matter of fact the visual art was not established as a fulltime profession in some societies and the artists had to depend upon other means for survival. Those who were adamant to devoting their life to art had to approach Horse Couch Painters or painters engaged in such menial jobs - for a daily wage - to learn painting. There was no Art School that a talented person could attend until the Thirteenth Century, when a formal teaching method to teach art was formulated.

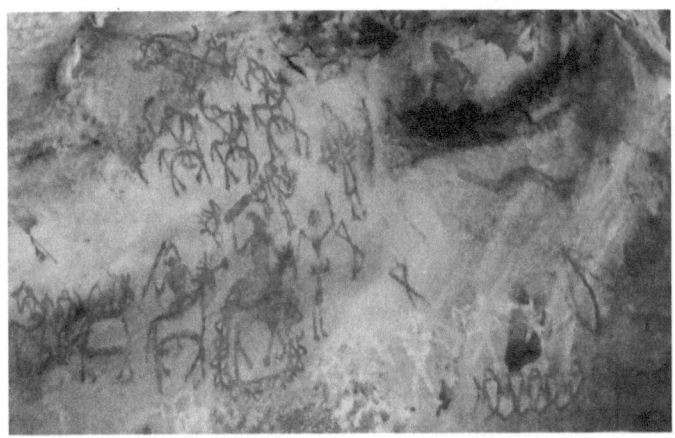

Celebration, animal and figures of men. Cave paintings from
Bhimbetka, Madhya Pradesh, India.

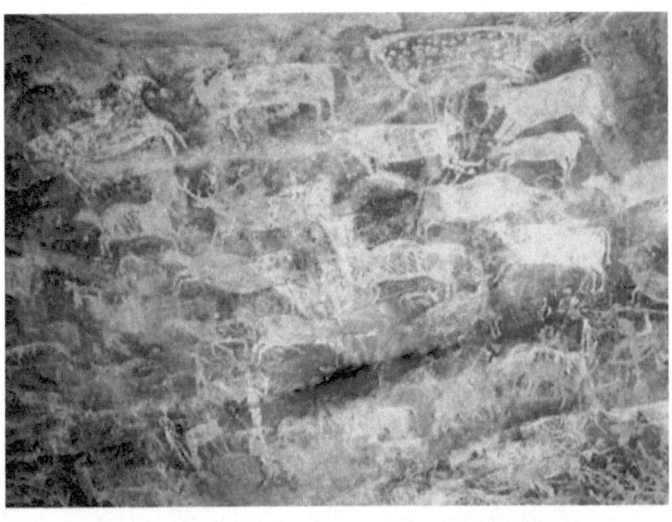

Animal figures. Cave painting from Bhimbetka, Madhya
Pradesh, India.

Notes

1. *Modernization- Modernization ideologically means the growth and existence of a progressive evolution from an ongoing widely accepted situation characterized by an orientation to the past. The word Modernization points not only the process of any change but also the responses of the beholders to that change.*

2. *Comparison- Comparison is the act of measuring differences of two or more materialistic or ideological potentials. It is enforced by evaluation of relevant characteristics of each potential accessible in the objectivity and differentiate similarities and differences with understanding on degrees of similarities and differences.*

3. *Research- Research is an innovative enquiry undertaken systematically which increases the thick scales of knowledge. Knowledge can be of any object or objectivity such as humans, culture and society, mechanisms, universe, organisms, etc. This knowledge is utilized to devise new applications. A research is under process when a question is posed, a collection of data is made for the use of answering a question and the answer is presented against question.*

4. *Experiment- An experiment is a modus operandi carried out to sustain, disprove, or substantiate a major dogma. Experiments bring understanding to reason and effect by representation of the nature of occurred result while a meticulous aspect is on exploitation. Nature of experimentation varies dynamically according to goal and scale. It is characterized by depending upon repetition of procedures without break on logical investigation of the outcomes.*

5. *Society-Society is gathering of different individuals with unique characteristics, but in persistent ideological interaction due to sharing of same spatial or social territory, and nourished with acceptance of similar political authority and majorly exposed cultural practice.*

6. *Artist-Artist is an individual occupied in action connected to create art, enthusiastic towards the arts. Individual signifying art objectivity is also denoted as artist. This word is used to denote an everyday practitioner in the visual art.*

7. *Imagination- This is the aptitude to turn out and replicate innovative core, humans and thoughts in the mind with no any direct input of the active senses. It is also explained as evolution of experiences in one's mind, which possibly be the re-creations of past experience such as flamboyant reminiscences with anticipated change. Also these can be fully imaginary and possibly unbelievable visuals. Thoughts supports create one information appropriate to find resolutions for tribulations. It is elementary for integration of understanding though the studious practice.*

8. *Creativity- This is an incidence of human beings by which something which had no previous existence and value is formed. Meaning of the formation may be absolutely an indescribable format or a physical object. Outcome may be evolution of an idea, growth of a scientific theory, formation of a musical composition, splatter of a joke, or ideological invention, as in the case of ideological when it may be an invention, a literary work, or a painting in physical objectivity.*

9. *Teaching- is a major activity of education and is the procedure of facilitating the understanding, or the*

attainment of knowledge, skills, values, beliefs, and habits. Methodologies of education include teaching, training, storytelling, coaching practicing, discussing and engage in directed research.

10. *Aesthetics*- is the stem of philosophical approach that deals with the character of beauty and taste.

References

1. *Roy C Craven, "Indian Art: A Concise History of Art". Published in 1976 by Thames and Hudson LTD, 252pages.*

2. *Benjamin Rowland, "The Pelican History of Art", Published in 1953 by Penguin Books, 512 pages.*

3. *Ananda K Coomarswamy, "History of Indian and Indonesian Art", Published in 1966, by Dover Publications Inc. New York. 295pages+XVIIIpages*

4. *Mathuram Bhoothalingam, "Temples of India, Myths and Legends", Published in 1986, by Publication Division, Ministry of Information and Broadcasting, Govt. of India.*

5. *C Sivaramamurti. "Indian Painting", Published in 1970 by National Book Trust, India, 132 pages.*

6. *Susan langer "Feeling and Form". Published October 11th 1977 by Pearson (first published 1977) 464 pages.*

7. *John Berger "Ways of seeing" BBC and Penguin Books. 1972. 180 Pages.*

8. *Sigmund Freud. "The Ego and the ID" Published 1960 by W.W. Norton & Company (NY) (first published 1923) 87 pages*

9. *Sigmund Freud, "The interpretation of Dreams" General press. 2019.*

India as a Sensitive Background for Art Education

Abstract: "It was fundamental for the diverse cultural institutions in India which managed establishments of inimitable education to society in the course of its constant existence even if this relation restricted all resources of fortitude during its subsistence, due to various factors but religious reasons were at prime. They continued teaching until got vanished from history, Hinduism, Buddhism, Brahmanism and Jainism are major among them and each of them introduced unique art education systems through ideological expansion and own survival. It was followed by Mughal Empire who encouraged Miniature Painting and Company School came into survival on prolongation to this which supported materialization of art activities to appeal Western sensibilities. Ravi Varma was totally criticized for his manifestations with oil painting: a Western device but Bengal school proved its name for being more Indian through their propaganda. The school established by Rabindranath Tagore at Santiniketan was an answer for many questions:

the new beginnings from here and with the emergence of Individual activities by various geniuses, a style accepted Pan Indian level began to stage in India and which led to new developments in Art education."

Key words: Colonial Period, Miniature Painting, Cave Paintings, Bengal School, Ravi Varma, Modern Schools.

Various cultural institutions in India managed establishments of unique education to society through its constant existence: this relation restricted all resources of endurance during its subsistence. It was essential for them to accept various circumstances presented by the society in which they phenomenally existed. The conditions to what they adjusted were of anonymous nature including religious, social, behavioral, geographical, historical, ethical, psychological, and economical aspects and so on. A major factor that affected and supported production of art in India is religious aspiration. Inventions of art objectivities by religious systems confirmed their productions not only by reflecting the visions of that particular religion, but insisting to stage its performance to make the viewers feel the necessity of spiritual ideals in society.[1] Each religious attitude dramatically placed on platform the necessity of its existence to the surrounding society as it is the most important element for social existence through their astonishing creations.

Following the above factors, the specialties and limitations of traditional art education systems lacked understanding about the requirements of the society in which they lived. Learning art directly from a teacher was a renowned feature. At the same time, the religious systems which were very robustly embedded in the Indian society, introduced a system highly appreciable for the subsistence and pronounce of religious extremity. Art was a highly cherished apparatus to edify religion, wherever it sprouted and remained subsistence strappingly. Taking shape of art objectivity was equal to the generation of a language for communication of ideals-the ideals of any mean. Those productions continued their teachings until they faced destruction by natural calamities, implementation of calculated enforcement by human generations or extinction due to self decomposition.

The acceptance of Buddhism and its establishment in India and elsewhere on earth opened new ways for the birth of valuable art and art education systems with reverberations worldwide. The religious beliefs and practices of cave Architects, Sculptors and Painters on Buddhism during its establishment, became the reason for the creation of world's best art objects, paintings, sculptures and architectural wonders. Based on Buddhism and utilizing all explorations of traditional possibilities, and the ideals of visual possibilities the religious systems that developed could astonish beholders of it from all generations. This was made possible by keeping the improvised visual habits and whole minded acceptance of all the limitations and explorations of all the possibilities by its creators the human beings. The successors materialistically witnessed and ideologically accepted the visual ideologies of their predecessors with mixed feelings. Each religious pedestal (founders and establishers) gave birth to aesthetic ideals in the directions they thought was the best for their religious, ideological and materialistic growth[2]. They introduced a social art education system anticipating innumerable possibilities for their own progress in the existing society, through the expansion of their religious ideologies.

During the rule of Mughal Empire a notable growth in artistic activities was noticed. With his warm hearted approaches to Aesthetic which means that Akbar the great proved his most loving personality towards fine arts among the rulers[3]. He loved all art forms and encouraged all creative activities. Hundreds of artists were appointed in his royal court to engage in painting and the most legendary priceless paintings in Indian miniature style with connections to Persia were painted during his period of rule. Another remarkable incident is that he brought some remarkably proven artists from the West to his court on invitation to interact with Indian artists. The European artists brought and introduced a new surface for painting, the canvas. They also came with a new medium, which was unknown to the Indians until then, the oil colors[4]. Many art historians commented in their writings, that introducing oil medium was the most relevant activity in modernization. Following the incident of introducing a new medium, there are evidences for the creation of images of Jesus and mother Maria in Miniature style during the 15th Century in the court of Akbar- a venue in history where the religious connotations and signatures turned meaningless. The efforts of Akbar to generate communication of Indian Artist with Western artists and bringing new ideologies to Indian art were considered as innovative by many Art Lovers, Art Historians and Art Practitioners.

There was another remarkable turn in effort on art education by the British in India. They initiated for creation of aesthetics suitable to western ideologies in India, which was largely accepted in the beginning and highly acclaimed.

It provided ambience to Indian artists by introducing creation of line drawing with following scales, anatomy and standards, water color soluble - wash techniques made illusion of thickness, perspective and three dimensional feelings. British focused on teaching these techniques to Indian traditional craft persons during the ages of Company School in India.[5]

Teaching western thoughts – the values of western art – to the Indian artist was completely a modernization procedure. When Westerners tried to imbibe new ideologies by introducing new values to the Indian platform, first they tried to identify eligible hands for transferring the basics. First of all they tried to find people from the families of artists who were Akbar's court painters. It took great effort to find the grandsons of old Miniature artists from the geographical areas where the traditional miniature artists made their settlements centuries' ago. It was a powerful ideology for creating transformation. Similarly foreign artists were introduced to Indian Royal Families, land owners, and rulers, and got their (Royal) images static as paintings done, as per special requirements of British East India Company, which was a great visionary act on educating Art.

Even if it was to establish their superiority and their psychic ego over Indian artists, in the name of documentation, European artists were appointed to create portraits of great land owners and the Royal family members turned as an innovative social art teaching program to the colonies of British and its people. Hundreds of European artists were appointed all over India, to portray powerful people, for creation of exact replica of places, buildings and incidents as part of making history. The entire procedures initiated a new kind of social art teaching and social art academic atmosphere. In this gene Thomas Daniel and William Daniel travelled along nook and corners of India, studied historical places, every details of it, by making replicas of landmarks, conducts of customs, religious diversity, living styles, mode of transportation, flora and fauna and so on[6]. It was a social art teaching program initiated by British to make Indians acknowledge how the art should work in any nation.

The break from the surroundings created the Indian artist Ravi Varma was an outstanding one. He was introduced to Oil color as an aftermath of British rule in India. I have already mentioned that British tried to establish art as tool to document Indian situations, including images of Royal family members. Theodor Jenson was a European Artist who was appointed to document images from members of the Royal Family in Travancore. He came with an introductory letter to the king of Travancore from Madras Resident of British. By then young Ravi Varma was already an artist at the Royal Court of Travancore under supervision of his own uncle, who acted as a guardian figure for Ravi Varma during his entire growth as an artist, Raja Raja Varma, approached Kingdom of Travancore to get Ravi Varma tuition in Oil Painting professionally from any of the visiting artists particularly from Theodor Jenson.

It was noted by an early art historian that Arumugham Pillai, then a court painter of Travancore, who was able to handle oil color, was not interested in teaching Ravi Varma oil medium, because he could visualize in Ravi Varma, a powerful opponent, who could appropriate and challenge his position as "great painter of Travancore". Simultaneously when Theodor Jenson came to Travancore with an order from the British Residency to portray the Royal Family of Travancore, Raja Raja Varma the guardian figure approached him through the Royal Family to teach Ravi Varma the usage of oil medium. But the highly considered artist Theodor Jenson had no special interest and pride in training oil painting to somebody particularly any Indian[7].

But with the interference of Royal Family in the matter, Ravi Varma was permitted to witness how Theodor Jenson mixed oil color. It has been previously noted by an art historian that this was the only training in oil medium accessed by Ravi Varma. The training of Ravi Varma was through engaging himself on numerous experiments in the new medium by trial and error. Ravi Varma succeeded in achieving a challenging mastery in the use of oil color by hard work and with use of his merit and inborn talent. By this challenging opportunity Ravi Varma could gather fame and recognition as the first modern Indian painter who could handle a western medium successfully and professionally in challenging manner. He made his name write in the history with sparkling alphabets.

During British rule, the Westerners, began Art and Craft educational centers in various cities including, Madras, Calcutta and Mumbai. These schools were initially for production of skilled laborers suitable for commercial purposes – production of utility objects, ornaments and jewelries, great architectures and so on, rather than individual artists. E.B. Havell, was working for renaissance in cloth weaving technology at Chennai in the beginning and was later appointed to work with Art Educational Institution at Calcutta[8]. There was a style of production known as South Kensington Style which was very popular. But nothing could remain persistent long against currents of changes that took formation since then.

Single mindedly the basic philosophy of "Bengal School" was laid by E.B. Havell, Ananda K Coomaraswamy and Abanindranath Tagore at the end of the 19th Century[9]. With the energy acquired from their surroundings, the artists of Bengal school involved in painting with the understanding that they are creating new art. Bengal school was innovative, outstanding and modern, when the historical atmosphere and society in which these activities were introduced are considered. Understanding the limitations of British Art Education system which followed South Kensington Style through European Models and teaching of Geometry, then Superintend of Calcutta School E B Havell experimented to teach with the introduction of Miniature style, Wash technique and purely Indian thoughts with the help of the cousins of Rabindranath Tagore.

Abanindranath Tagore, the founder of the Indian Wash style was appointed as the main recourse person and major teacher there. With confidence, E B Havell was able to sell off the European models brought from home town for teaching in Calcutta. Soon E B Havell was called back from Britain to return due to the "Psychological Problem" from which suffering. After a long time of 'treatment' E B Havell could come to India only to pack for hometown permanently. Again a new principal was appointed at the Calcutta School, said to be a stickler to discipline, Mr. Percy Brown[10]. Soon after the arrival of the new teacher, Abanindranath Tagore left his teaching assignments there. But the Bengal school continued its growth in to a Pan Indian level with establishment of its Indian terms and terminologies.

During the days of Bengal famine, the society was facing various economic failure issues including starvation. "Chitto Prasad" a Naxalite[11] activist from the villages of West Bengal acted powerfully through woodcut prints. He visualized the human conditions during starvation and transferred it to outer world. Situated in the village "Lal Bandh", "Somnath Hore" was his follower, studied the technique from Chitto Prasad and continued his communication span for human generations with a most appreciable humanistic manner. The style of public teaching was absurd and arrogant to the then ruling commune but it showed pathways to a new generation, an art teaching style and methodology. It was rash, rude and turmoil to consider the development of a teaching system, but it renders soft modules of affectionate potentials when its humanitarian grounds are under consideration. This unique use of a creative medium, in a very open manner, for social purpose takes space here due to its social content.

On closure of Bengal School activities in Calcutta School, Poet Rabindranath Tagore began Kalabhawana within Visvabharati University his dream space of education. The visions of Rabindranath Tagore were entirely different from the ones of his nephews. He questioned them for their over refinement and repetitive qualities for which they were trying to moot up in the banner of renaissance. The establishment of Rabindranath Tagore as an art enthusiast and supporter contributed largely to the establishment of modernism. He ridiculed his nephews - for laying back in the Indian style, rendering from Mughal period, making wash paintings-instead of learning developments in the West-and provoked them to work towards new tendencies of Modernism in the

West. He tried to initiate a teaching system in his school with the presence and teachings of Nandalal Bose the preeminent disciple of Abanindranath. Finally after visiting Europe again and visits of Okakura Kakuzo from Japan, Rabindranath Tagore himself began to paint, and established as an artist.

Stella Kramrisch was invited by the philosopher, poet and artist Rabindranath Tagore[12] to Santiniketan during the end of the 1920s. It was the time when the genius among the ordinary began to think the necessity of building awareness in art history among the Indian Artists. It was the announcement of modern age in art education in Indian continent.

In 1950s the well known artist N S Bendre[13] together with the university administrator Markhandeya Bhatt initiated studies on art at M S University of Baroda during its foundation workout. It was much before, with the interest of famous sculptor D P Roychowdhury, modernization was initiated at Madras. Slowly the school at Madras reached a completely and ideologically higher status since the arrival of K C S Paniker as its head. K C Paniker[14] was a visionary of art education and creatively involved in art creation and establishment of artist's profession. The teaching of art in a professional level was begun by artist B C Sanyal at Delhi in the early 1970s and he was able to establish art education there elaborately. Later by the end of 1980s, by the arrival of O P Sharma[15] to head the institution made remarkable changes in its teaching styles. O P Sharma established Bauhaus initiatives since he studied art from Bauhaus school background. Initiatives of all art institutions in India within past twenty five years have made remarkable changes in the growth of Art Education. The art education in India took rebirth with capabilities of international acceptance along with growth of art educational institutions in various cities of India.

One of the most important facts was the understanding about the newly developed art in the Indian society. It included acknowledgements of expansion in art education system in countries abroad. Several artists of Indian origin were unhappy about the teaching in the existing art educational institutions and began to acquire education from institutions established abroad. With their return, they created an elaborate functional atmosphere on joint efforts with natively educated artists. The artists happened to be settled in big cities, began to work jointly with the understanding of established ideologies, new philosophical contents and several active groups that were born. Progressive artists groups in Mumbai, Chennai, Calcutta and Delhi were established in newer and higher levels which were unique in history. These groups were established with new ideologies in visionary habits and rendered a new aesthetic vision to the society in which they survived. Establishment of such groups gave an outlook on the society on general awareness of understanding towards art. Also the efforts of numerous Individual artists who worked regularly and enthusiastically for ideological and practical enhancement of Art and Art education is also mentionable here.

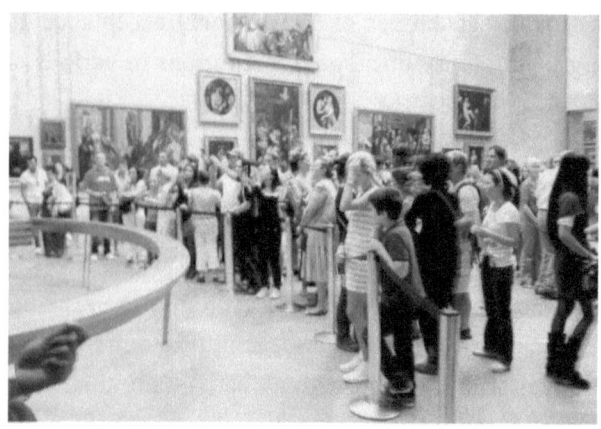

Picture shows the viewers of "Monalisa" in the gallery at Luvre Museum, Paris which ensures teaching Art to Public in a moderate level. It continues for the past several centuries to many thousands of publics who visit, teaching how art should be. Photography by Artist Babu Namboodiri K, 2011.

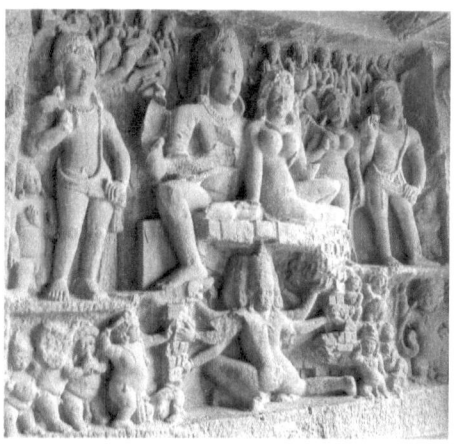

Sculpture from Ellora Cave: It continued its art teaching for past several centuries with its religious aspirations, also with enquiring minute scopes of it with diversities. Famed as the most important venue of representation with intensive theatricality. The Ravana shaking Kailasa.

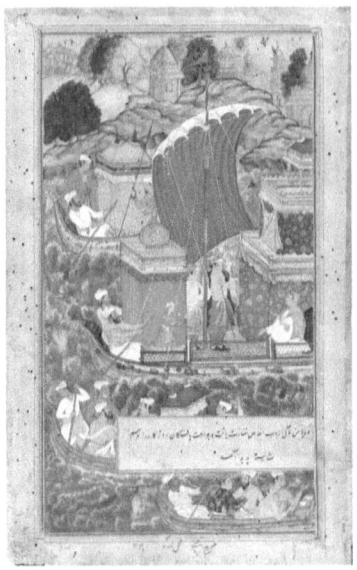

Akbar's mother crossing river in night, painting from Royal court of
Akbar- Akbar Nama. Established manner of Miniature Painting.

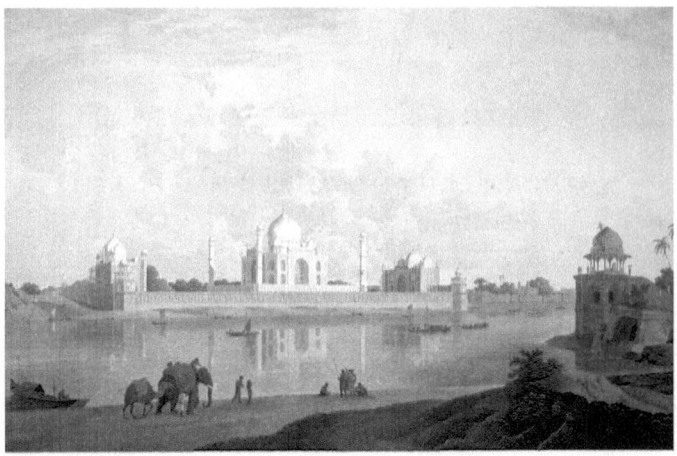

Company School painting by William Daniel, Moderate attempt to
teach art to Indians in a European manner.

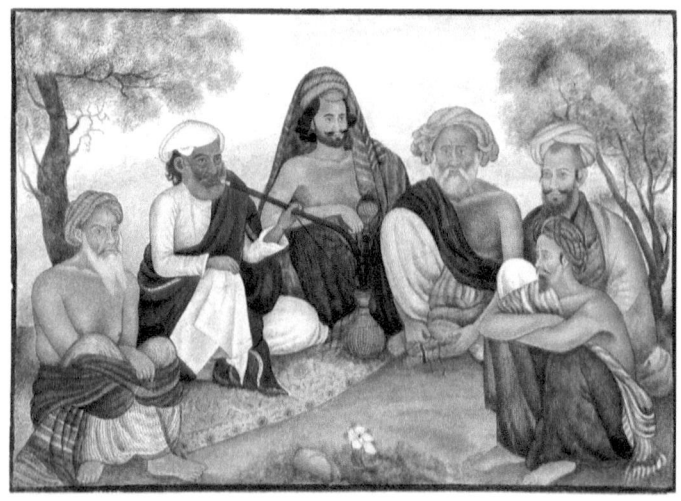

**Khan Bahadur Khan with men of his clan, Indian attempt
to satisfy the British tastes.**

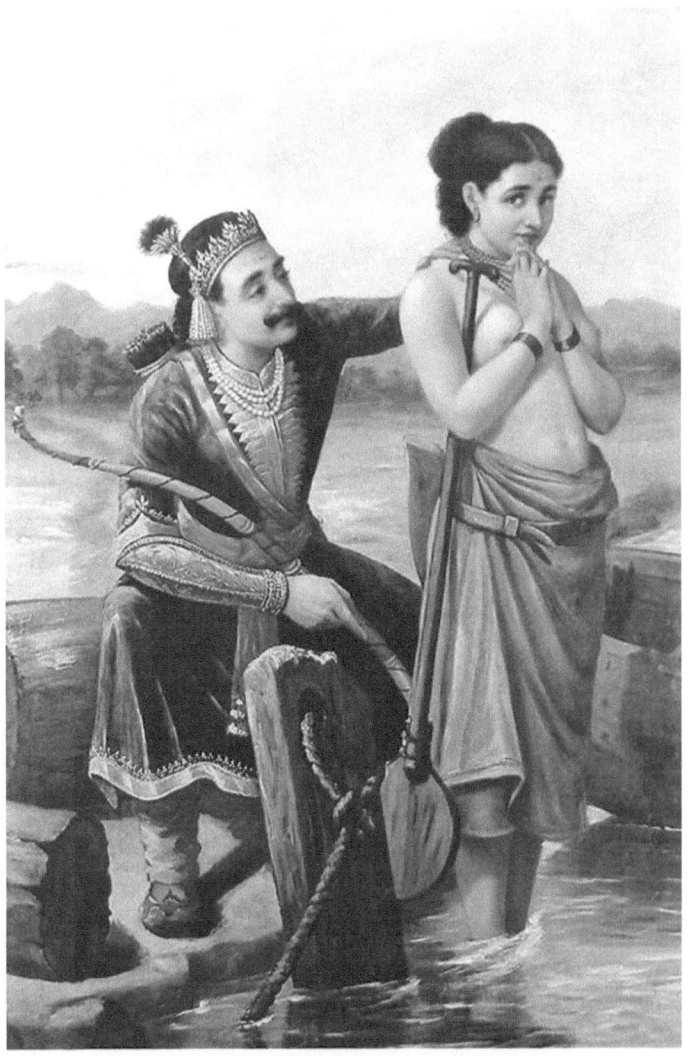

"Santanu and Satyavati" Painting by Ravi Varma.

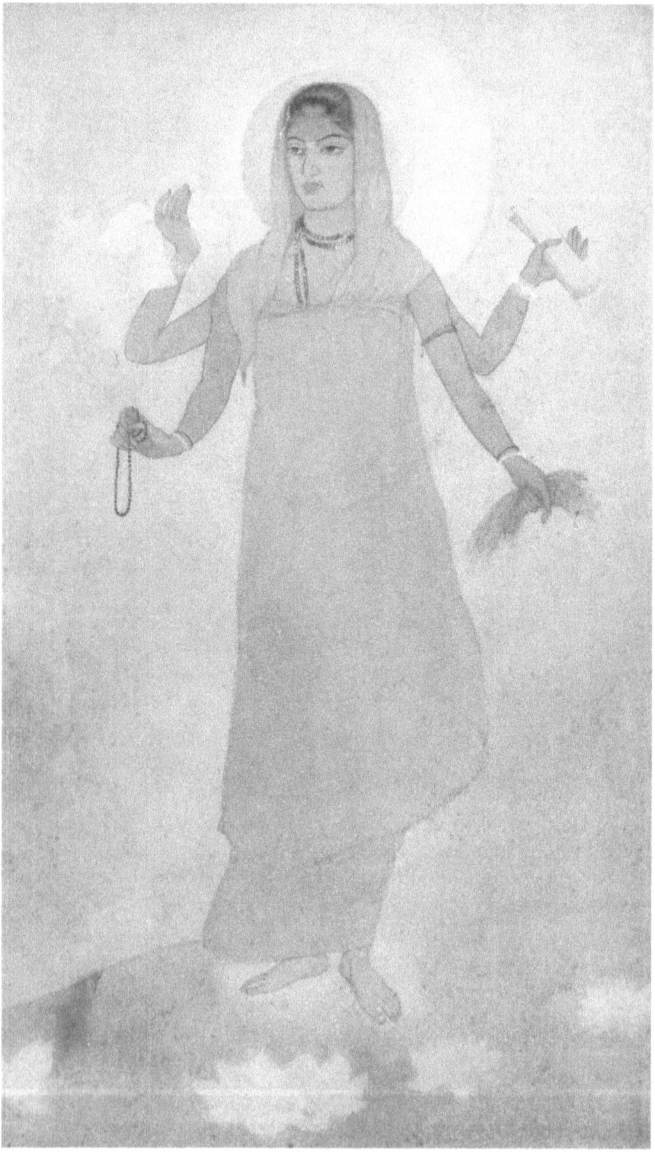

"Bharat Mata" Bengal School painting, attributed to
Abanindranath Tagore.

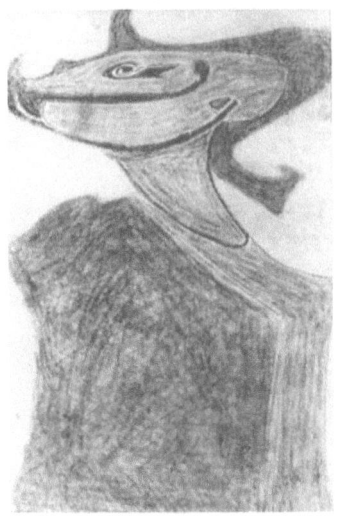

A creation by Artist Rabindranath Tagore. Experimenting oneself
to paint.

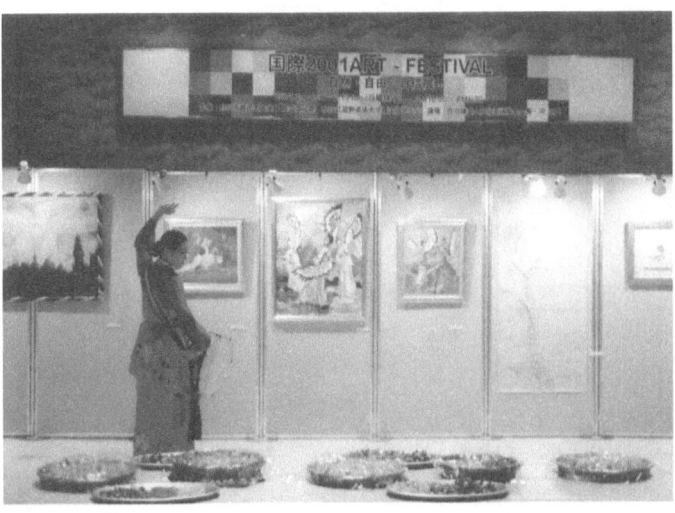

Contemprary Art Galleries often turns venues for teaching new
visions on art to its viewers. Photography by Artist Cha Kyung Dai,
Busan Korea during show at Tokyo in Silk Gallery, 2001.

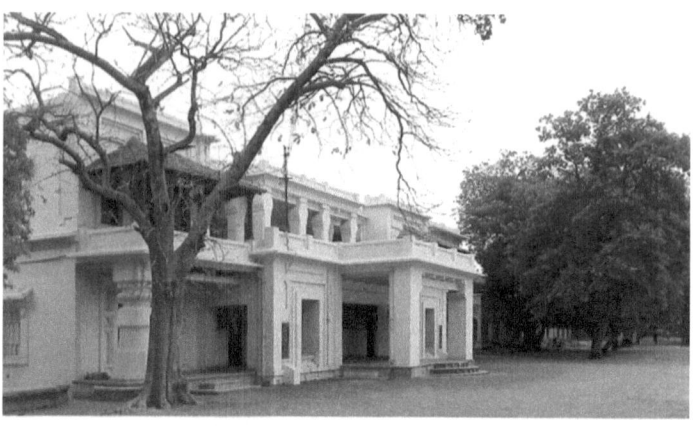

An immediate venue for launch of various changes, apt centre for experimental and ideological teaching initiatives on Art. Building for Fine Arts Faculty at Santiniketan of Rabindranath Tagore.

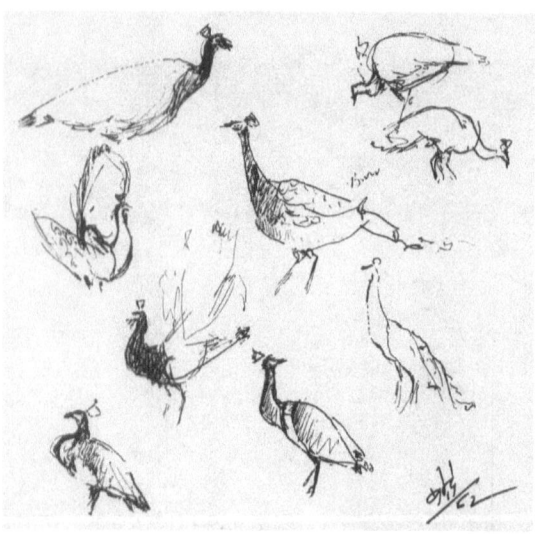

Educating art with Professionalism. Sketch of Artist N S Bendre 1962, reproduced to silk screen print later. Collection by Artist Babu Namboodiri K,

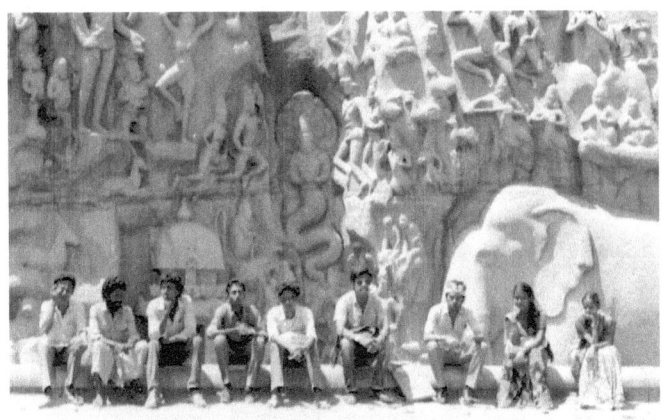

Visual art teaching finds its own methods. Artist Nitai Majumdar on visit to Descends of Ganges at Mahabalipuram with his desciples. Teaching on the way. Photography by Artist Babu Namboodiri K 1986.

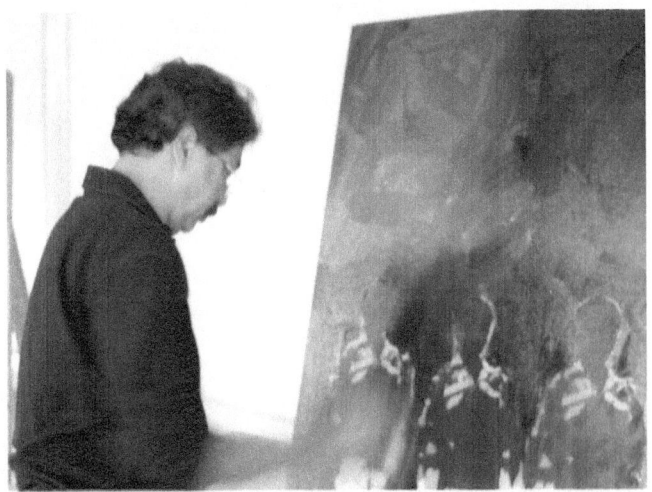

Demonstrating Art practice at certain venues turns an avenue for education. Late Artist, Yusaf Arackal at work during a demo. Photography by Artist Babu Namboodiri K. 2006.

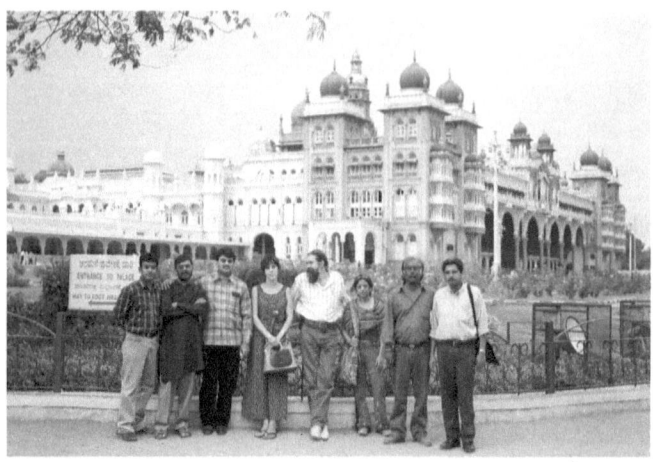

Sharing new lessons and ideologies in one of the rarest occasions. Artists from United Kingdom, Russia and Europe sharing with Indian artists and officials during 11th Triennale India in 2006.'

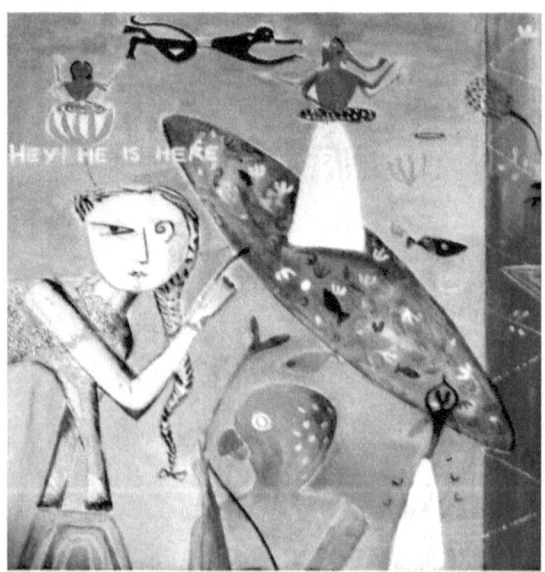

What to teach anybody Art? Painting By artist Muralidharan K, Chennai, Photography by Artist Babu Namboodiri K 2006.

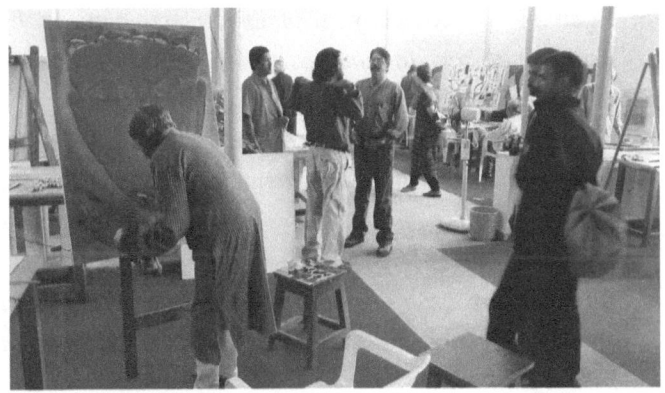

Working in groups motivates creation and communication between artists and viewers. Artists and viewers during an artist's camp at Bangalore in 2007. Photography by Artist Babu Namboodiri K. 2006.

Notes

1. *Differences between ideological consumption of Buddhist, Brahmanic, Jain Buddhist ideologies during various centuries of creation of caves in Ajanta, Ellora and temples in various parts of the Globe are on reference here.,*

2. *Referring the stylistic differences between visuals in the form of sculptures and paintings in caves made during various centuries in Ajanta, Ellora, Elephanta, or anywhere else.*

3. *The Royal court of Akbar included thousands of artists to make paintings in Miniature style. Akbar was a true lover of art and there are no equals for him that took birth in the globe.*

4. *Many historians' points to the fact that Akbar made initiatives to establish new medium, oil on canvas, invited western artists to his court to teach oil painting to our painters.*

5. *Referring to company school painters brought by British and how Indians learned art during company establishment.*

6. *There were many hundreds of people who travelled all along India, visualized the activities, Places, Festivals, Behavior, Kings, Customs, Jewelries and so on. Daniells are just example.*

7. *All major art historians in the past stated and discussed about emergence of Ravi Varma as the First Modern Indian painter.*

8. *E. B. Havell tried his level best to replace art tendencies prevailed in India, replaced British models from the art school, appointed people favoring new art practice with Indian elements etc during his principal ship at Calcutta School etc and gained success to an appreciable level.*

9. *E B Havell tried to bring revelations through implementing new teaching styles with seeking from Abanindranath Tagore for practical support and Ananda K Coomaraswamy for philosophical support.*

10. *Mr. Percy Brown was a differently person by temperament, a stickler to discipline, who objected the freedom enjoyed by Abanindranath Tagore and his students.*

11. *Chittoprasad taught Samnath Hore and was appointed for visual reporting from various parts of Bengal during Famine.*

12. *Rabindranath Tagore invited several personalities from various parts of the globe to South Verandhah of Jorasanko Family house in Bengal, and later to Santiniketan after establishment of it, to find remarkable changes in Philosophic approaches towards the progress*

in Art, Literature, music, Theatre and culture generally and it turned fruitful.

13. Artist/Painter N S Bendre was the founder of Faculty of Fine arts in Baroda M S University.

14. K C S Panicker was the student of D P Roy Choudhury and later Principal of College of Fine Arts at Chennai. He took initiations to begin Cholamandal Artists village in a later period of his life and became leader of the movement there.

15. O Pm Sharma was the Principal of College of Art, New Delhi late 80s and early 90s who made ample efforts to build a new school there.

References

Selected Reading

1. *Ananda K Coomarswamy, "History of Indian and Indonesian Art", Published in 1966, by Dover Publications Inc. New York. 295pages XVIIIpages*

2. *Mathuram Bhoothalingam, "Temples of India, Myths and Legends", Published in 1986, by Publication Division, Ministry of Information and Broadcasting, Govt. of India.*

3. *C Sivaramamurti. "Indian Painting", Published in 1970 by National Book Trust, India, 132 pages.*

4. *Vasudeva Agrawala, "The Heritage of Indian Art, A Pictorial Presentation". Published in 1986 by Publication Division, Govt. of India. 186 pages.*

5. *Articles by various writers on "Modernism and Bombay Progressive Art Group and Group 1890" in Lalitkala Contemporary 2, 22 and 31 in 1963, 1978 and 1990 respectively by Central Lalitkala Academi, New Delhi.*

6. *Various Writers, "Bendre: The Painter and the Person", Published in 1990 by Bendre Foundation for art and culture and the Indus Corporation, 210 pages.*

7. *Mildred Archer, "India and British Portraiture, 1770-1825", Published in 1979 by Oxford University Press.296pages.*

8. *R P Gupta, "Some British and European Painters in India, 1760-1850". Published in 1979 by Times of India in its Annual.*

9. *Philip S Rawson, edited by Pierre Tisme, "Indian Painting" Published in 1970 by Universe Books Inc. New York.*

10. *Chintamonikar, Yogesh Chandra Bagal and MukulDey"School of Industrial Archool of Art 1865, College of Art and Craft 1951 at Calcutta", published in 1966 by College of Art Calcutta. 217pages.*

11. *Prodosh Das Gupta, "Calcutta Group Manifesto", Published in 1970 by Artist's Group at Calcutta.*

12. *Articles in publication "Trends Art Magazine' published from Cholalmandalam Artists Village, Chennai.*

Modernization in Art Education as Measured with Ancient Parameters to Current

Abstract: Creating abilities in his students who represents unique circumstances- for the creation of substantial aesthetic potentials in work of art is the major role of an art teacher. There was a face to face interaction between teacher and student in traditional set up. But it was unavoidable to accept a more efficient mode of interaction when the demands of art education in the society increased into many folds. Place to place from time to time, art education took immense of changes beginning from face to face transaction of methodologies and ideologies to introduction of a particular stylish schooling. The Bauhaus system of teaching developed in Germany was suppressed by Nazi activists during the Second World War. Then after, it took an interesting turn by spreading its style of activities all over the world.

Key words: Tradition, Religion, Art Practice, Lives, Art History, Public Art Teaching, Bauhaus.

Traditionally, the role of an art teacher is to engage in creation of art along with his students, so that the students could learn the technical aspects of creative art production, and ensure engagement in art creation until the students could make own abilities stable for creation, create art with sound self understanding and establish as an artist to the existing society with pride. It offered the students the opportunity to learn directly from his teacher, taking time as long as he needs and engage himself in projects with the knowledge that he acquired during his studies. This style of teaching was ideologically new when it took shape. It can be assumed that the artists who were convinced to share their understandings to the one, who persistently demanded for his working knowledge to get transferred, might have followed similar procedures to make their followers stable and worth productive. Similarly the same method might have adapted even when the number of pupil increased many folds. So that when the transfer process of working knowledge on regular basis began by the established one, the beholder (of working knowledge) might have initiated the process based on the then established conventional outlines.[1]

But the number of Individual people who engaged in acquiring training in a specific active area of one's interest in fine arts had increased soon, due to its immediate social acceptance. Teaching according to the demands of the apprentice was a modern perception then. Apart from acquiring the most basic knowledge, the followers adapted the moral principles of their God fathers of wisdom during practice of their own lives. The scholarly began to accept the visions and manners of their coach and they began to maintain certain characteristics unique in their creative production for lifelong, which led to the formation of similar creeds of production, later established and identified as schools.

Even if the stylistic approach of art teaching system was related to any one of the Social, Personal or Ritualistic altitudes, and teaching was performed in Religious altitude too. Each religious commune was competing with the other to acquire their own style of teaching art since art was socially accepted as a means of ideological communication for an observer. As an endeavor of laying foundation, establishing religions and their thought processes even through architecture the ancient followed unique identical features in typical residential buildings, prayer houses, and common buildings. The unique aesthetic properties accommodated in them helped the growth of art among common people and expanded its vivacious usage into many folds. The religious fundamentals intended for the growth of religious altitude that focused on establishment of their own ideologies, supported the art practice in the typical manner for their progression. They vehemently insisted for precision in the creators vision, on the philosophic viewpoints urged by religion to which they belonged to and confirmed that the creativity persistently suffered by becoming slaves to their religion. When such creators fully devoted their minds and physical manifestation for the creation of such religious art, they reflected that what they produced were realistic status of religion to which they are committed. In later sophisticated studies it is pointed out that these ideologies are of contradicting nature.

But in that epoch, the creative art production centre in Italy marked deeply, their presence with prominence and it require special attention historically due to its sound attempts to support architects, painters, sculptors, and aestheticians like Michelangelo[2]. The school of Florence

(Florentine School)[3] supported by Medici Family[4] was basically supported and promoted by Christianity[5] and it's stank believers. Due to the creators deep rooted believes in religious practice and the issues of materialistic existence, their slavery to the socially well renowned religions were unavoidable. So with the art creators' anonymous quantities of creative pursuits, the art practice with aesthetic achievement entered in to a new age. 'Giorgio Vasari'[6] the aesthetician and primary historian opened important doors to the changes in conceiving art practice studiously.

Giorgio Vasari had also acquired his wisdom in art practice from the surroundings of Florence School. He turned extra ordinary due to the unique efforts he made, and was considered as the first notable individual in the history to be considered by future theorists through the powerful literary representation 'Lives'. On completion of studies at Florence, Vasari was wandering through various kingdoms in Europe, particularly in Italy. Slowly he was able to establish his name as a painter and architect. Centuries later his literary contribution 'Lives'[7] got widely accepted and was well received globally among aestheticians and historians with the understanding towards its limitations.

Giorgio Vasari attracted fame as an architect for buildings like 'Palazzo Vechio' and continued with artistic activities. He published second edition of 'Lives' in 1555. The imaginary elements in the descriptions of Vasari, made the 'Lives' romantic, rather than affirming it historical or factual. He may have not got widely accepted as an art historian in the advent of the current phenomenal ideologies, but his contributions will remain vital forever because he coined the term "Art History" by writing about lives of artists. From the day 'Lives' was created, study of art history begun and with the adaption and establishment of continuous and progressive changes it developed into an unavoidable part of art education.

The existence of art activities and its establishment made a kind of 'public art teaching' around the globe. The society began to accept certain parameters (measuring scales) established by artists in its hinterland. The gathering of artists and the supporters of art began to develop scaling standards for evaluating art and related activities within the circumstances where they survived. The society made understandings to evaluate art of each time span with scales that developed within each period. The Royal Art society[8] of England and Salon de Art, Paris[9] were two institutions where activities existed with historical importance in the end of 19th century. During their existence, both took very important roles in social art teaching. Placing themselves in very important turning points of the history, both institutions made several revolutionary changes in teaching art the society through individuals. On compulsion and appeal of artists who got rejected from the annual Exhibition of Salon de Art, Paris in 1863, another exhibition was conducted by Napoleon-III against its annual exhibition. This exhibition gathered popularity in the globe as 'Salon de Refuses'[10] which marked the rebellion of artists against Salon (any such phenomena) and its scaling parameters. After this exhibition, the works those exhibited in Paris Salon or else were never the same. The social changes inspired various artists of the society and their unique productions established as many 'isms' in a short span of time. Each "isms"[11] and periodical differentiations made it possible to teach art following their own methodologies to the immediate society which differs in each period of revelation.

It has been noted by various art historians that the changes in the methodologies of art taught by various art institutions that took shape since 10th century and continued during various time spans in history. These institutions were largely influenced from time to time by developments in the society, and according to the changes it adapted. Each institution held a new unique idea which they began functioning and conceived changes afterwards. It is worth to note that the basic characteristics of all institutions had similarities in function without seeking ideas from the place wherever in the globe. These institutions provided systematic art learning initiatives wherever they were situated. Also, they promoted similar interests in teaching art to the forth coming generations.

By its very existence, BAUHAUS[12] school challenged all the prevailing styles in teaching art and established a new one. Centered in various cities of Germany, Bauhaus school initiated new teaching methods. Study is generally explained as visualization of ideas through sketch followed by drawing. Instead of copying earlier productions, Bauhaus concentrated on real studies directly from objects and objectivities, engaged in studies of living organisms, natural locations, vegetation, and surrounding nature which were part of the new education style. The new school basically taught what design is and meant by it, and gave an important position for learning History of Art and Aesthetics in art education.

All the credits of introducing a new style in this format went to Photographer Walter Gropius,[13] artist/painter Paul Klee[14] and Architect Moholy Naggy.[15] It began to take shape just before First World War but the anti-human approaches[16] in the Second World War[17] stopped this initiative. Many

Bauhaus school artists suffered at the hands of Nazi[18] activists. Artists (any creative personality) were treated like guinea pigs; by using them for unauthorized biological experimentations. Some artists got colors directly injected to their eyes on experimentation, to see what happens to the color of their eyes, some of them were treated as psycho patients and some others were violently tortured: made naked in rows, lead to gas chambers and put to death. Artists and all sorts of genius ran away from Germany to safer parts of the globe. With the advent of Hitler[19], Bauhaus school genius scattered all over the globe. The scattered mass, explored their situations, and they began to establish ideologies of Bauhaus wherever they were. The existence and establishment of Bauhaus supported the growth of new schools in similar lines. The establishment of new style of Bauhaus had fascinated world minds since its very beginning. Hence the influence of Bauhaus school in the global system of art education is stamped evidently forever.

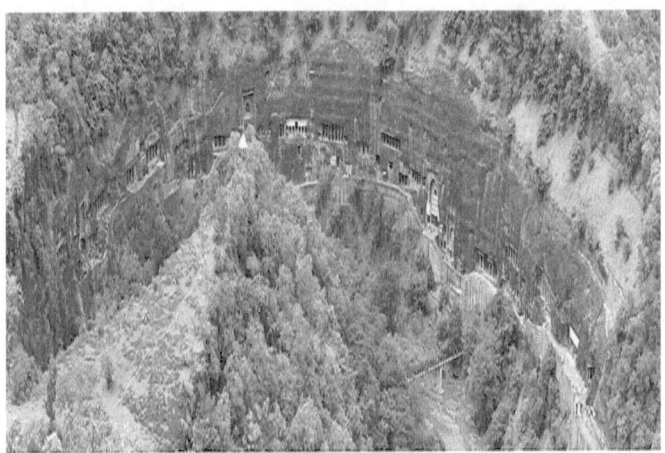

Ajanta Caves · reflects persisting religious affinities on creativity.

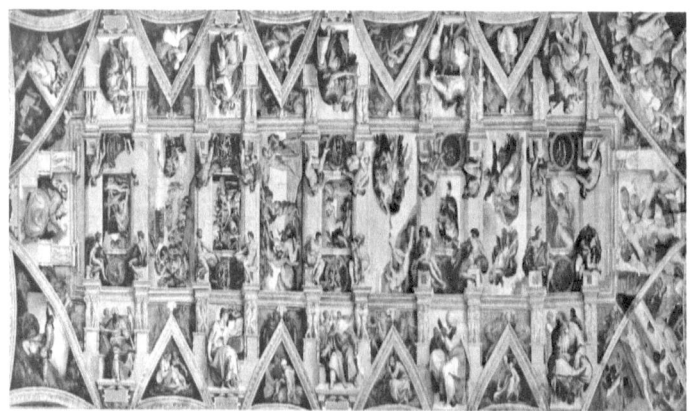

Michelangelo - The painted ceiling of Sistine Chapel with religion and creed based bias.

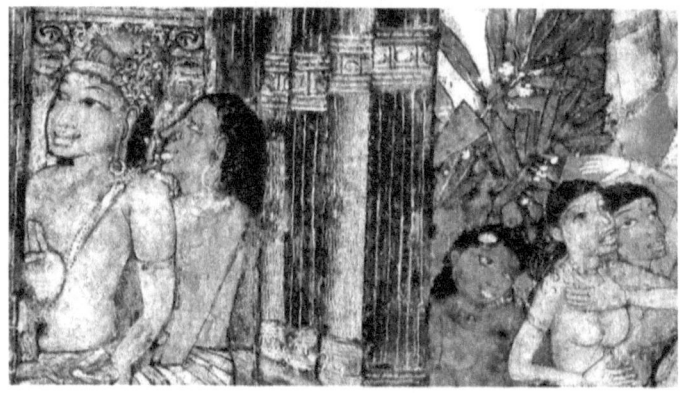

Painting at Ajanta Cave - confirming the religious affinities of the creative sensibilities.

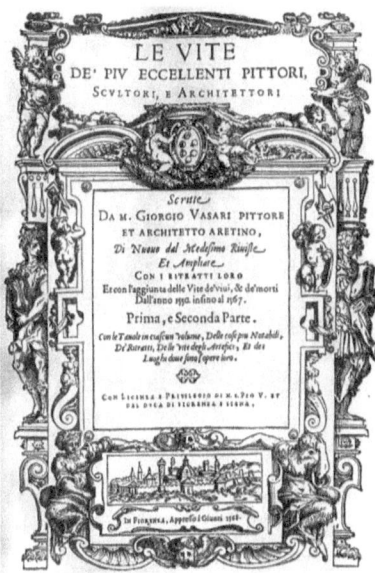

Cover page of the first sincere recording on artists "Lives" (Title page of the 1568 edition of Le Vite) by GiorgioVasari.

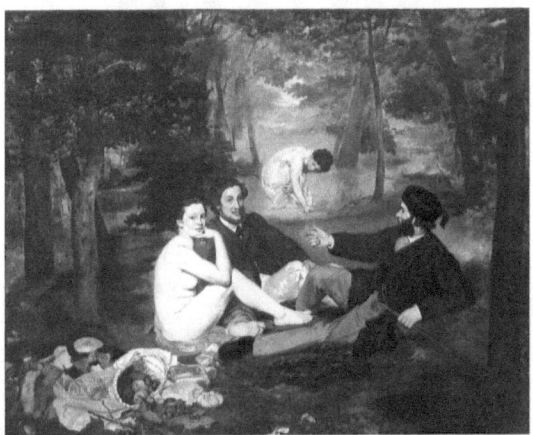

Painting of Impressionist-Édouard Manet, The Luncheon on the Grass (Le déjeuner sur l'herbe),1863. was an exhibit with Salon de refuses first exhibition.

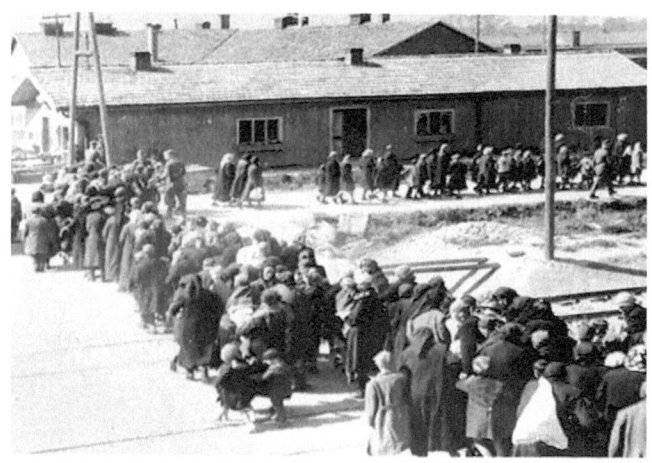

Nazi workout of Holocast. Crowd of Jews including women and children lead in a que to kill in Gas Chambers. A shocking memory of the past.

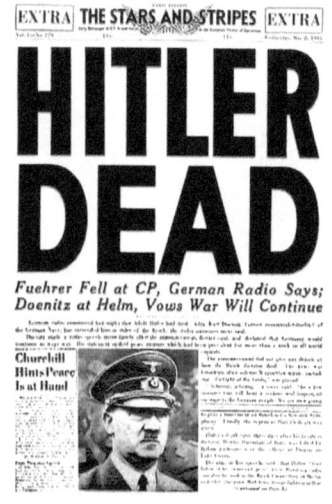

An end to state of cruelty to Humanitarian concepts and vanishing of only Hitler. The Stars and Stripes magazine celebrates the Death of "A Hitler"

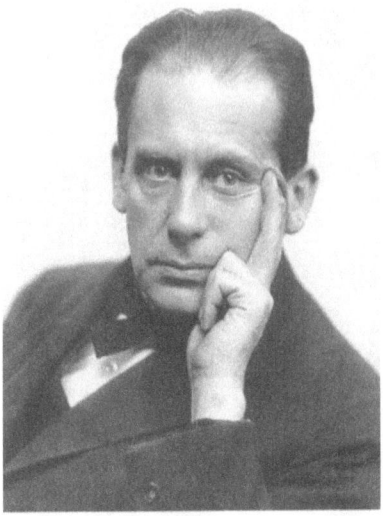

Walter Gropius, The founder of Bauhaus School in Germany.

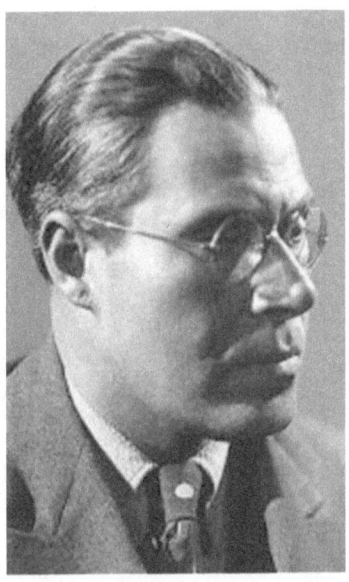

Moholy Naggy. A Phenomenal figure of Bauhaus and a
constructivist artist himself.

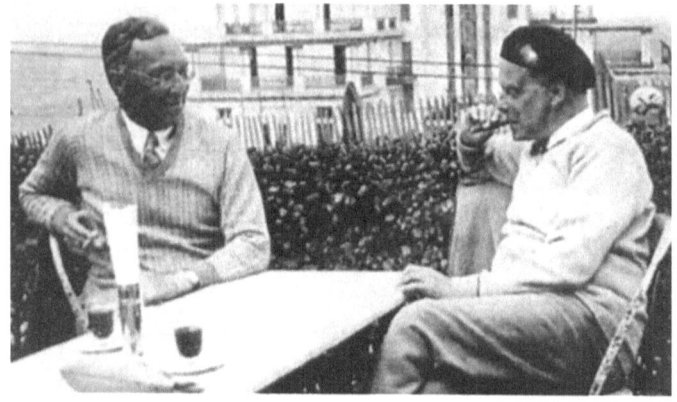

Sharing of thoughtful moments by two challenging personalities, artists Kandinsky and Paul Klee at Bauhaus.

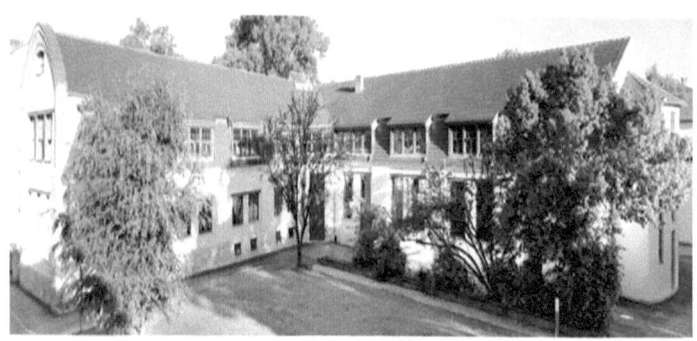

Bauhaus faculty of Fine Arts and design, Desseau.

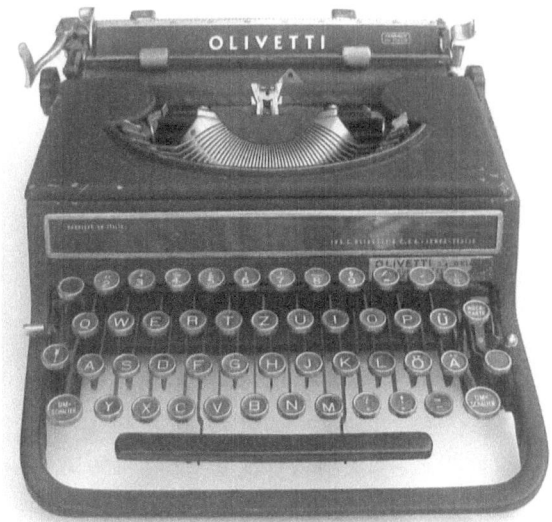

Bauhaus design of Olivetti Type writer

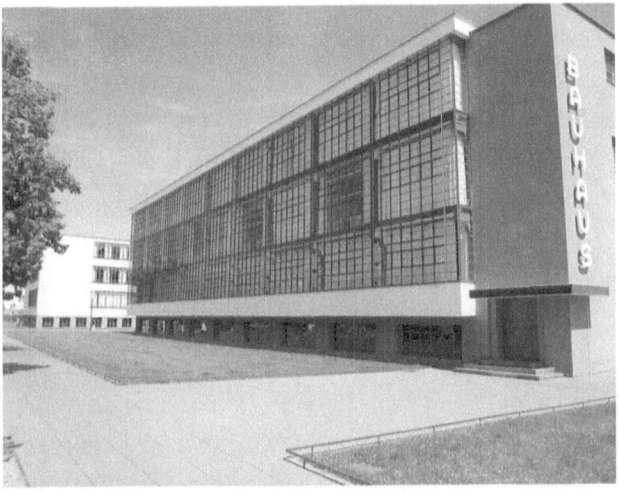

Bauhaus School new building with stylistic alphabets in Bauhaus style in Germany.

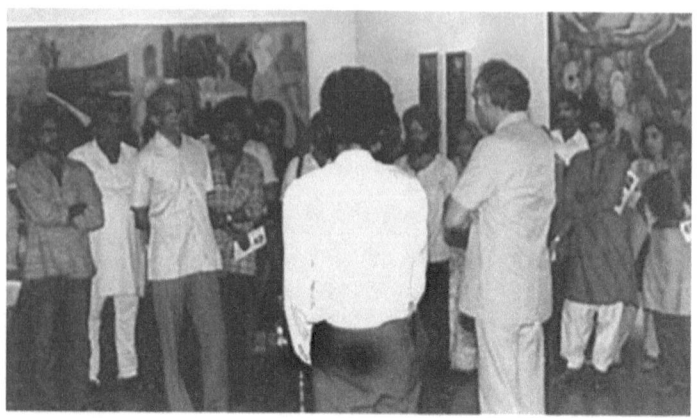

Artist Om Prakash Sharma (a Bauhaus School alumni) shares with his students in New Delhi during gallery visit while he was Principal College of Art, New Delhi 1990.

Notes

1. *According to ancient Indian system it is known as Gurukulam where the students go and stay with their teacher for studies.*

2. **Michelangelo:** *Michelangelo di Lodovico Buonarroti Simoni: Italian (6 March 1475 – 18 February 1564), popular with only the very word Michelangelo, born in the Republic of Florence, Italy was a phenomenal success in sculpture, painting, architecture and poetry during High Renaissance. He made unparallel influence of positive energy on the development of Western art, equal to Leonardo da Vinci, and was also sponsored by Medici family the supreme support for art forever in the globe.*

3. **School of Florentine: Florentine painting** *or the* **Florentine School** *refers to artists who worked with the naturalistic style developed in the 14th Century Florence.*

Fra Angelico, Botticelli, Filippo Lippi, the Ghirlandaio family, Masolino, and Masaccio were some of the best known painters of the earlier Florentine School. High Renaissance took its shape in Florence as a continuation of creative efforts of these artists. In the early 16th Century the largest commissions ever attracted artists including Michelangelo and Raphael and they moved to Rome.

4. ***Medici Family:*** *15th century onwards this banking family(Medici Bank) gathered reputation and sponsored several artists in Europe, could produce four Popes in the Catholic Church, made two women of their family the queens of France, and acquired the hereditary title the Duke of the Florence.*

5. ***Christianity:*** *Christian is said to be the world's largest religion with about 2.4 billion followers based on the life and teachings of Jesus of Nazareth and consider that Jesus is the Christ.*

6. ***Giorgio Vasari:*** *(30 July 1511 – 27 June 1574) was an Italian painter, architect, writer, and historian belonged to Florentine school, and wrote "Lives of the Most Excellent Painters, Sculptors, and Architects" which is considered as the ideological foundation of art-historical writing. "*

7. ***Lives:*** *Giorgio Vasari wrote "Lives" and tried to include all developments of Renaissance in a superficial nature was first published in 1550.*

8. ***Royal Art Society:*** *England. London-based, British organization - Founded in 1754 by William Shipley as the Society for the encouragement of Arts, Manufactures and Commercial aspirations. As it was granted Royal patronage in 1847, it acquired right to use the term Royal.*

9. ***Salon De Art, Paris:*** *The "Académie royale de peinture et de sculpture" the royally sanctioned French institution of art patronage, (a part of the Académie des beaux-arts) held its first semi-public art exhibition at the Salon Carré in 1667 to display of the work of recent graduates of the École des Beaux-Arts.*

10. ***Salon De Refuses:*** *It was general that all the artists submit their art works for selection of Jurry conducted by Salon de Paris each year. Salon jury including Alexandre Cabanel and Franz Xaver Winterhalter, refused to exhibit two thirds of the art works submitted by artists in 1863, which included the works of Gustave Courbet, Édouard Manet, Camille Pissarro and Johan Jongkind. The rejected artists and their friends protested which reached Emperor Napoleon III, who decided that the works of art which were refused must be displayed in another part of the Palace of Industry.*

11. ***Isms:*** *Various changes focused on particular subjects and subjectivities took place in art are known as Isms like Impressionism, Post Impressionism, Pointalism, Expressionism, Abstract Expressionism, Fauvism, Cubism, Constructivism, Dadaism, Sur realism and so on.*

12. ***Bauhaus:*** *The Staatliches Bauhaus generally famed as Bauhaus, is an Art School in Germany operated since 1919 to 1933 which unified the crafts and the fine arts.*

13. ***Walter Gropius:*** *(18 May 1883 – 5 July 1969) O5riginally from Belgium, German Architect Walter Adolph Georg Gropius) was a leading architect of International style found the Bauhaus School initially at Weimar in1919. In a later period he could build it into the world-famous Bauhaus which attracted faculty t including artists*

and aestheticians including Paul Klee, Johannes Itten, Josef Albers, Herbert Bayer, László Moholy-Nagy, Otto Bartning and Wassily Kandinsky

14. **Artist Paul Klee:** *who was considered both as German and as Swiss painter (18 December 1879 - 29 June 1940) was born in Munchenbuchsee, Switzerland. He was largely influenced by various art movements like expressionism, cubism, surrealism and a student of oriental ism. Along with companion the Russian painter Wassily Kandinsky, he taught at the German Bauhaus school of art, design and architecture. He was driven with dry humor in painting and followed a childlike perspective reflected his personal moods and attitudes with inbuilt rhythm.*

15. **Moholy Naggy:** *Moholy-Nagy was born in Hungary to a Jewish family, worked with Bauhaus along with walter groupies and Paul Klee the artist. After the coming up of Nazis with power in 1933, he was unable to survive in Germany as he was a foreigner found teaching job at Royal College of Art much later*

16. **Anti Human Approaches of Second World War II:.** *By state of Great War emerged during World War II, which made direct involvement of 100 million people connected with 30 different countries. Human life in all sense got seriously affected and all humanitarian means were destructed in establishment of military power- 70 to 85 million fatalities of World War II was the deadliest conflict in human history ever.*

17. **Second World War:** *Japan and China were on War each other by 1937. World War begun in 1st September 1939 when Germany invaded Poland and UK joined to support the weaker to war against Germany. By*

continuous War enforcement Germany conquered major areas of continental Europe since late 1939 to early 1941, and formed the Axis alliance (Alignment agreement) with Italy and Japan. Germany and the Soviet Union partitioned and annexed territories of their European neighbors, Poland, Finland, Romania and the Baltic states Under the Molotov–Ribbentrop Pact of August 1939. The war continued primarily between the European Axis powers and the British Empire. It was followed by War in the Balkans, the aerial Battle of Britain, the Blitz, and the long Battle of the Atlantic. The European Axis powers launched an invasion of the Soviet Union, opening the largest land theatre of war in history on 22 June 1941. This Eastern Front trapped the Axis, most crucially the German Wehrmacht, in a war of attrition. Japan launched a surprise attack on the United States as well as European colonies in the Pacific In December 1941. Following an immediate U.S. declaration of war against Japan, supported by one from Great Britain, the European Axis powers quickly declared war on the U.S. in solidarity with their Japanese ally. Rapid Japanese conquests over much of the Western Pacific ensued, perceived by many in Asia as liberation from Western dominance and resulting in the support of several armies from defeated territories.

18. **Nazi:** *German Workers Party* Soon after joining of Hitler in it was renamed to National German Workers Party and begun to recognize as Nazi Party. He could adopt a version of the ancient symbol hakenkreuz or hooked cross as its emblem printed in white circle on a red background. This swastika took a shocking effect in representing symbolic power in the years followed

19. **Hitler:** *Adolf Hitler the chief of Nazi party was the most dominant and disreputable totalitarian of 20th century globe. He capitalized on economic means, popular unhappiness and political internal friction to take unconditional power in Germany beginning in 1933. Germany's incursion of Poland in 1939 led to the outbreak of World War II, and by 1941 Nazi armed forces had engaged much of Europe. Hitler's abusive anti - Semitism and irrational chase of Aryan dominance triggered the murder of more than 6 million Jews, along with other fatalities of the Holocaust. Adolf Hitler the most notorious dictator of 20th Century, committed suicide in a Berlin dugout in April 1945 after the gush of war turned against* him.

References

Selected Readings

1. Alan Bowennes, "Modern European Art". World of Art Pub. By Themes and Hudson, London. 1972. 224 Pages.
2. Arthur Coestler, "The Act of Creation". Pub. by Picador Pan books L.t.D, 1970, 501pages.
3. Clieve bell, "Art" Roopa Paper back, Pub. Bu Roopa & Co, New York, 2002, 292 Pages.
4. Herbert Read, "A concise History of Modern Art" World of Art, pub. by Thames and Hudson, New York, 1968, 1974,1986, 396 Pages.
5. Ritwik Sanyal "Philosophy of Music" Pub. By T V Kunhikrishnan for Somenia Publication. Private LTD. Bombay. 1999, Pages 142.
6. Roy C Craven, "Indian Art: A Concise History of Art". Published in 1976 by Thames and Hudson LTD, 252pages.

7. Benjamin Rowland, "The Pelican History of Art", Published in 1953 by Penguin Books, 512 pages.

8. H.H. Arnason, "History of Modern Art, Painting, Sculpture, Architecture" Pub. Bu Harry N Abrams Incorporated, New York, 1977, 740 Pages.

9. David Lodge (edited) "Modern criticism and Theory" Pub. By Longman London and New York, 1998, 1991. 467 Pages.

10. Essays of Swami Vivekananda. Published in various books, publications mainly by Vivekananda Kendras established in various places.

11. Immanuel Kant, Observations in the feeling of Beautiful and Sublime, Translated by John T Goldthwaith, University of California Press, Berkeley, Los Angeles, London.

12. Immanuel Kant. Religion within the boundary of Pure Reason By Immanuel Kant, Translated by J.W. Semple Advocate. Edinburgh, Printed By Thomas Allan & Co, 265, High Street. Pages 276.

Role of E B Havell on Manifestation of Indian Ideals in Art Education

Abstract: *Due to the attitudes held in initiatives from the British Colony rule and its officials, the art education in India and art practice were facing various problems with identity and originality. Many arts schools began to function with the inspirations from the great exhibition of 1851 with the initiatives of private individuals and collaborations for the enhancement of art activities in India but could not take any solid action towards improvement of it. E B Havell, a British art official took initiative to change the situations responsibly and challengingly by seeking help from Indian art enthusiasts. The career of E B Havell was cut short by the British, citing a mental breakdown and never returned to India after 1908. But the initiatives of Indian ideals continued vigorously by his Indian counterparts in this objectivity.*

Key words: Colonial Art, Abanindranath Tagore, E B Havell, Sir Jamshetjee Jeejeebhoy, Calcutta School of Art, Ananda K Coomaraswamy, Bengal School.

Ernest Binfield Havell (16 September 1861 – 31 December 1934), who was well known in the name E.B. Havell, was a powerful art administrator, Art Historian and was in India for more than two decades connected with these activities. He is the author of numerous books on Indian art and architecture. Belonging to Havell family of artists and art educators, he was the principal of the Government School of Art, Calcutta from 1896 to 1905, where, with companionship of artists in Tagore Family, especially with Abanindranath Tagore, he managed to develop a style of art and art education based on Indian models rather than the then established Western models, which led to the foundation of the art. This study focuses on the various elements that supported him and evaluates the kind of modernism he could insist in art education and art practice, as well as how he maintained the various relevant situations and tackled his involvement logically to fit to an earnest art enthusiast.

The art situation in India which exposed and maintained the status of art to the public as a colony of British, and then the pathetic colonial political situations covered art in India were always discussed in meetings of British colonial administrators in several occasions in the past. Art established in the name of Indian art had high influence of traditional Indian Art including miniature painting traditions of 15th century India. At the same time even the exhibitions and other programs organized by colonial government failed to support and improve the degrading situations due to the un reliable management. "These surveys and exhibitions made decay of Indian Art manufacturers glaringly clear, which had already set in due to the free flow of cheaper European Machine made goods which were greatly in demand by the indigenous population"[1]. "The Revenue and Agriculture Department of the Imperial Government made a resolution in 1883 on museums and exhibitions with regard to the improvement of art manufacturers of India and promotion of trade in them within India as well as in foreign countries."[2] With notion to eradicate vulgar situations, an exhibition was set up in 1883, which was organized with headship of T H Hendley and was assisted by principals of art schools Bombay and Lahore, J Griffiths and J L Kippling respectively. The editor for the journal - to record and establish related facts – which started to issue from 1883, was J L Kipling. It included the details of the collections of Calcutta museum which was meant to act as an idealistic sample room for the materials collected in annual exhibition at Calcutta, which in effect intended to collect high quality materials for Indian Section at International exhibitions. In this connection, the last major exhibition held in 1902 was at Delhi Durbar initiated by Lord Curzon under the colonial government[3].

"To maintain, restore and improve the application of oriental art to industry and manufacture"[4] many arts schools began to function with the inspirations from the great exhibition of 1851 with the initiatives of private individuals and collaborations,[5] but the colonial government did not take any direct management of the same. Even though four art schools at various cities - Bombay, Calcutta, Madras and Lahore began to function before 1883, with the aim to cultivate fine arts, but only got secondary priority. The art education in India was a matter of discussion and frank debate at a Royal Society of Arts meeting in London in 1909, in which E B Havell was the principal speaker. In speech he focused on the anomalous and wavery policy towards art teaching in India. It was noted that art grew as a part of their tradition in Europe but the status of art in India could not be similar to it. A reason for this failure was the establishment of art schools in India without necessary planning for any kind of such understanding and they followed the basics of British pattern of art education that kept a distance from the idealistic roots. The artists who studied in these art schools were not capable of tackling various issues impeding their professional progress due to lack of education. No serious analysis was conducted for improvements since the inception of them until the situations went catastrophic. A number of art enthusiasts including Alexander Cunningham, Lord Curzon, John Marshal, Lady Herringham, T. H Hendley, J Griffiths, J. L Kipling, Green Wood, Cecil Burns, Gladstone Solomon, Robert Chishom, Dr. Hunter, Higgins, Terry, H.H Locke, Annoda Prasad Bagchi, Lord Norhbrook, Percy Brown, Colonel E. Goodwinn, Justice Hodgson Pratt, Rajendralala Mitra, and several other British, Europen and Indian[5] trained art enthusiasts were working in India as Gods men for the enrichment of India's art education and the salvation of Indian Art. It should be noted that it passed many decades with highly involved art practice and teaching by 1880. Starting from the great exhibition of 1851, after thirty years of hectic activities in art, the colony government could only make one progressive result. It instituted regular course of drawing by replicating the South Kensington style[6] in National Art School, Bombay in 1880. It was later established as J J School of Art,[7] on remembrance of Sir Jamshetjee Jeejeebhoy, who offered Rs.100000/-to East India Company in 1854 for the materialization of establishing the school. It reflects how seriously and generously the Indians thought of developing art situation in India and the how the situation was penetrated by the Western art enthusiasts to build their art dreams in the land of Miniature schools. It points out that how mindlessly the British Empire who had only calculations of economical and lucrative business terms stood feeling less in such cultural matters.

Abanindranath the cousin of Rabindranath, was friendly with E B Havell and Dr. Ananda K Coomaraswamy[8] due to various cultural reasons, the cultural exchange between them was philosophical, aesthetical, logical and much more than any kind of camaraderie. Abanindranath Tagore was an alumnus of the Calcutta School, in his studious period he was taught western art practice by various teachers like O Khiladi and others. The family traits at Jorasanko family house of Tagore considered learning art and practicing culture of the most effective and sensitive education a human can afford. When a Western but sincere open personality like E B Havell began to appear in Indian Scenareo, it was not Rabindranath Tagore, Gaganendranath Tagore or Abanindranath Tagore were supporting E B Havell but a whole of the Calcutta geniuses were welcoming the initiatives against practices of a European School in the land of miniature tradition.

It was in 1896, E B Havell took over the charge as Principal at Calcutta School of Art, and the art school and gallery moved over to its new and commodious premises near the Indian Museum. During the principalship of E B Havell, Abanindranath Tagore was appointed to teach at Calcutta School and the bond with such personality began to make strong cultural initiatives in the Indian scenario. With interaction of philosophical genius Ananda K Coomaraswamy and others, Abanindranath Tagore was much maneuver to initiate Indian style painting which announced the propaganda of Bengal School. When Nationalism, Indianism and Revivalism were caught into culturally nourished brains they began to act accurately without surrendering themselves to own personal limitations. Abanindranath Tagore tried to alter destiny of the Indian artists by modeling himself as an Indian Artist in every sense through his art practice with Indian Visual ideologies that were established since centuries ago in Indian corners such as Royal Kingdoms of Rajasthan, Pahari, and Mughal[9]. E B Havell the Employee of British colony rule, personality who understood the necessity of changes in entire teaching system and began to act accordingly.

E B Havell who came after a decades of experience as the Head of Madras School of Art, was really unhappy in the British style art education system, observed and noted the weakness that "The study of Design, the foundation of all art, was entirely ignored and throughout the general drawing and painting classes, the worst traditions of English Provincial art school forty years ago, were followed. There were no general classes for practical geometry, mechanical drawing and perspective. Oriental Art was more or less ignored, thereby taking the Indian art students in a wrong direction. Besides this there was no regular examination system for the issue of certificates to the deserving students"[10]. E B Havell was unhappy with the new strategical move to divide the school into two distinct divisions, 1. Industrial Arts, and 2. Fine Arts.

As an effort to correct the situations, E B Havell proposed teachings of Oriental arts in the first division of the school. according to the establishers view "The object of having an art gallery attached to an art school is to mould the taste and direct the imagination of the students by means of the works of art exhibited and yet though the students were Indian and the object of the school was, or rather should have been, the improvement of Indian Art and not the Introduction of European Art, the collection of pictures which was gathered together for the Art Gallery consisted almost entirely of copies of the old Italian and early English School, while Indian Art was practically neglected"[10]. With the spirit of recreating the system E B Havel, re organized the Art Gallery of Indian Museum, he started to procure specimens of Industrial Art for the gallery to serve as samples for new style education that he planned to stage there. The art gallery was reorganized in three sections, 1. Art applied to industry, 2. Architecture and architectural decoration, and 3. Fine Arts. He made several introductions like teachings in several new craft techniques, Fresco paintings, Stained glass for windows, lacquer work and stenciling focusing employment opportunities for students when they complete their studies. New style let the teaching of figure and nature study continue in the Fine Arts section, also where he thought direct acquaintance of Indian examples would be beneficial. E B Havell went on leave for a year in 1902[11]. On his arrival after one year he continued his attitude for change more powerfully.

He tried to rewrite the entire teaching style of the Calcutta school and went even to sell off British Models brought from England to teach students the stylistic art the British planned for them, with the approval from Lord Curzon. He established there a gallery of Indian art by replacing European pictures with fresh purchase of Indian Painting. He persuaded Abanindranath Tagore to join the staff and placed him as the Vice Principal of the school in 1905. The changes he adapted made arrogance from various corners including agitation from students of the school and E B Havell was largely punished for the crucial job he plat formed vigorously[11]. The career of E B Havell was cut short from British part, said to be due to mental breakdown and he never returned to India after 1908.

Abanindranath continued teaching at Calcutta school till 1915, until he developed strong differences with British Principal Percy Brown who did not like the freedom enjoyed by the students of Abanindranath Tagore. He resigned from Calcutta School but continued teaching at Indian Society of Oriental Art at Calcutta. Among his students at Calcutta School, Surendranath Ganguly, Nandalal Bose, Asitkumar Haldar, Samarendranath Gupta, Shailendranathdey, Hakim Md. Khan, Venkattappa, and Promode Kumar Chakraborti famed as practitioners and propagators of Bengal School. Nandalal Bose became faculty at Santiniketan, Asitkumar Haldar at Lucknow, Samarendranath Gupta at Lahore, Shailendranath Dey at Jaipur, Venkattappa at Mysore[12]. The period of teachings by Abanindranath Tagore in Calcutta with premises of Indian Society of Oriental Art after resigning from Calcutta school was also remarkable due to the establishment of Bengal School simultaneously with art activities of Nandalal Bose at Santiniketan[13].

Conclusion: It was already noted above that E B Havell was relieved from his job as the Principal of College of Art Calcutta and the dispute at Royal society of Arts meeting in London in which the principal speaker had been E B Havell. As he was already out of the arena, he could courageously expose the disasters of the Government Policy with regard to the emphasis on Indian Art Education. He rudely criticized against "double standards[14] with which art manufactures and the conventional arts of painting and sculptures were viewed and projected. The disagreement of E B Havell was on policies that categorizes Indian artist to second rank by placing him as craftsperson and not as an intellectual even after he proved his worth as an individual artist of merit". He argued that if Indian Artistic Geniuses had found that the expression in producing articles of beauty for domestic use how could they have failed in the case of "Fine Arts", as if they were guided by two separate aesthetic philosophies"[15]. He questioned the logic of considering Indian artists as craft persons and guided him to respect their handicrafts, by imbibing only conventional forms in creation. He rebelled against policy of British to consider artists of colonies inferior and directed them to absorb Western ideals in the name of civilizing them (with great artistic ideals of the west) to make them capable for the production of genuine outcomes. According to E B Havell, it was useless of the art school studies remained in the schools, unless and until the link between the subjects taught in the schools were directly linked to industry. He directly announced his anguish towards the situation that all the pass outs of the art schools targeted to maintain abilities to become portrait artists due to its demand. Surely this kind of argument from a highly considered personality of their own nation against conventional the thoughts made reformatory results in their behavioral attitudes further.

Courtesy: Images' Common files widely available are on use.

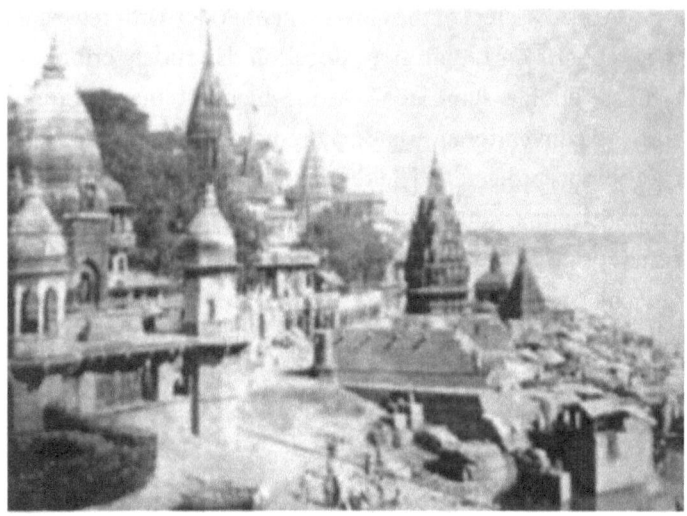

Banaras Ghatts, Engraving by E B Havell

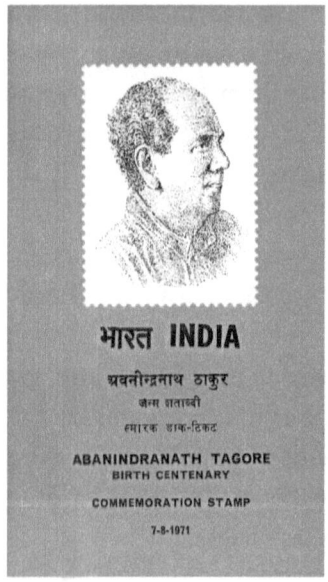

Abanindranath Tagore.

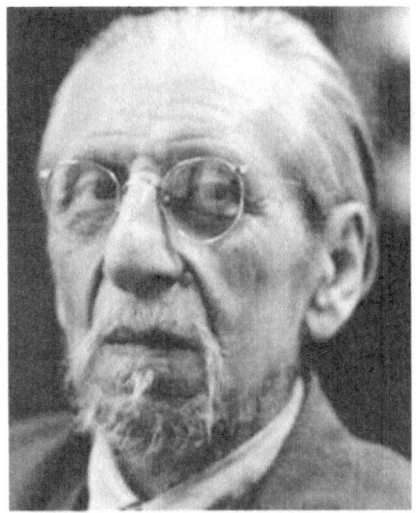

Ananda Kentish Coomaraswamy.

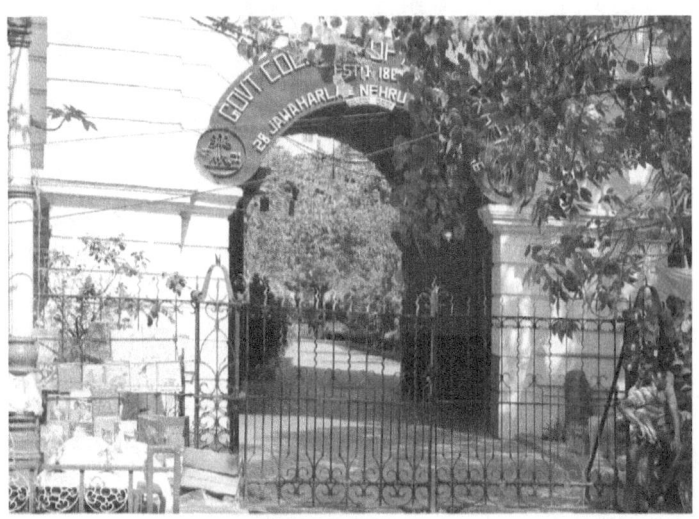

School of art, Calcutta.

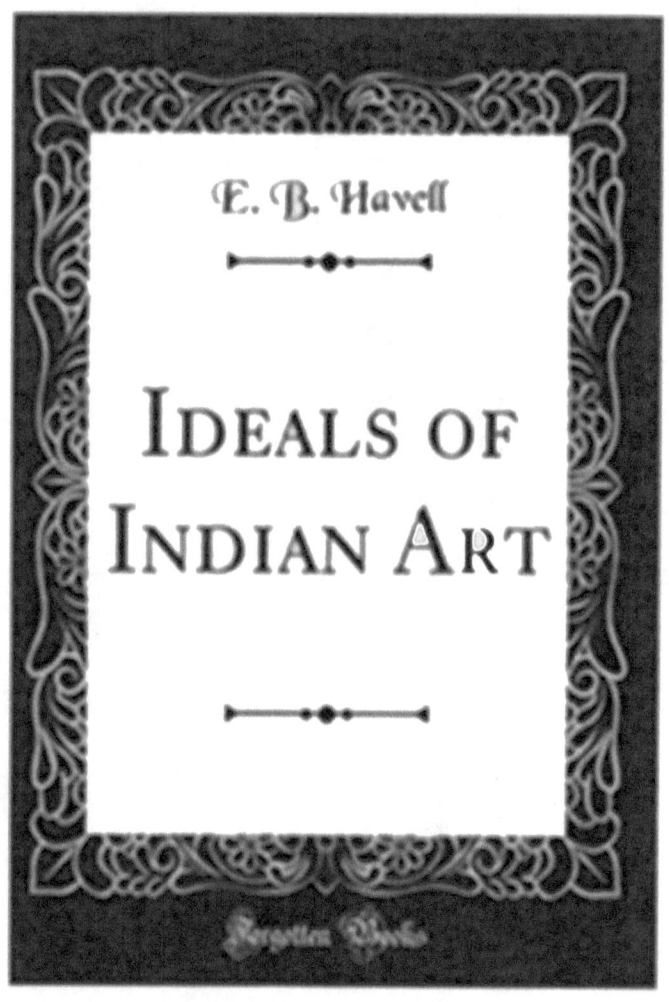

Ideals of Indian Art. Cover of book written by E B Havell.

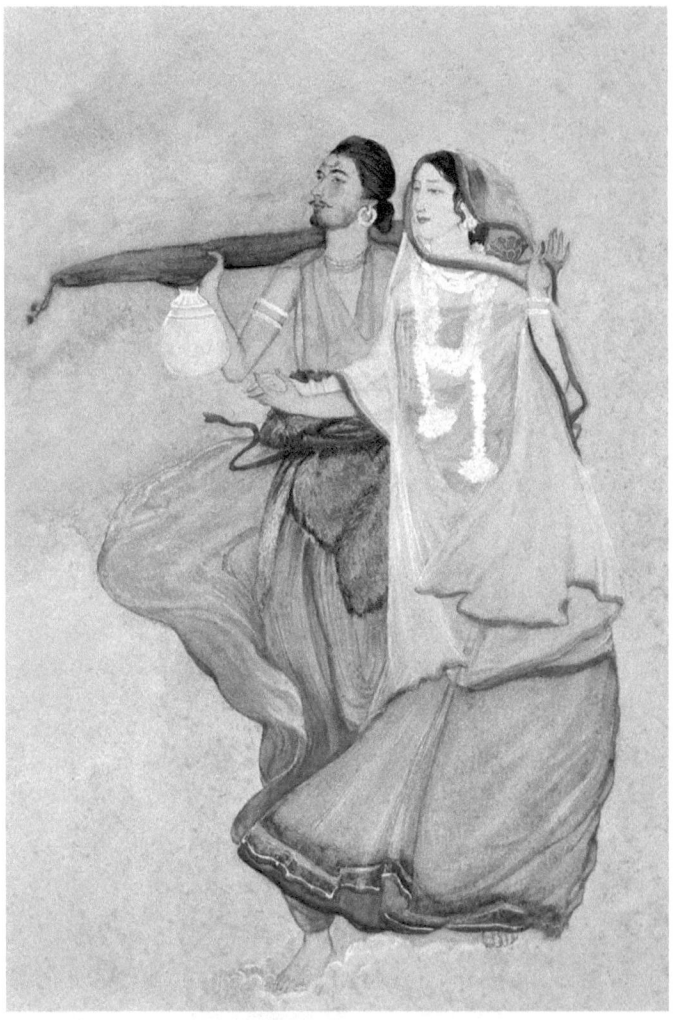

"Apsaras in the air" Perfect application of self invented "Wash" technique on paper. Painting by Abanindranath Tagore.

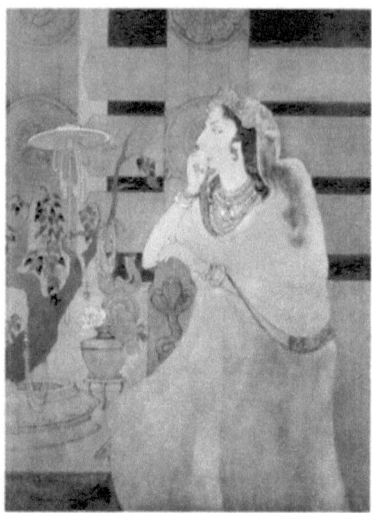

"The Queen of Asoka" Utilized historical revelations romantically.
Painting by Abanindranath Tagore.

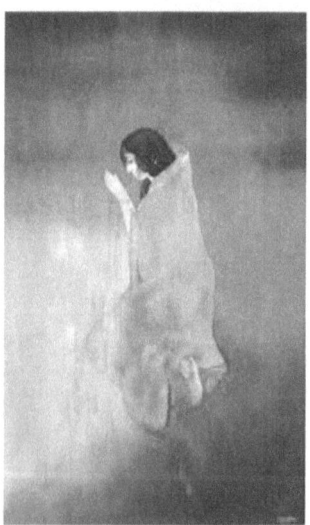

"Sati". Thoughtful use of social element in wide representation.
Painting by Nandalal Bose.

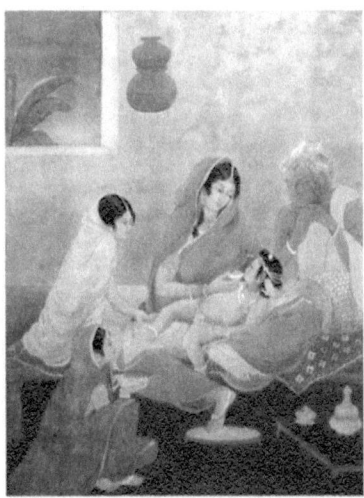

"Maternal nursing to a God" wide expression of narrative qualities.
Painting by Asit Kumar Haldar.

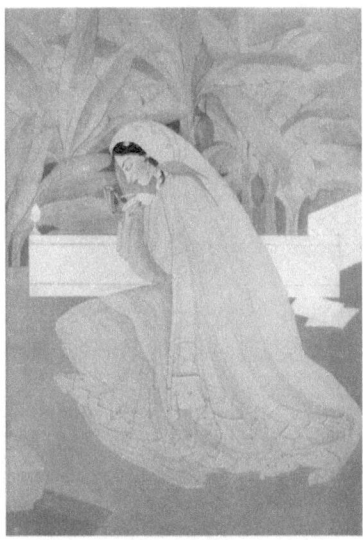

"Beauty in action". Working beyond cultural diversities gathered a
national appreciation. Painting by A R Chughtai.

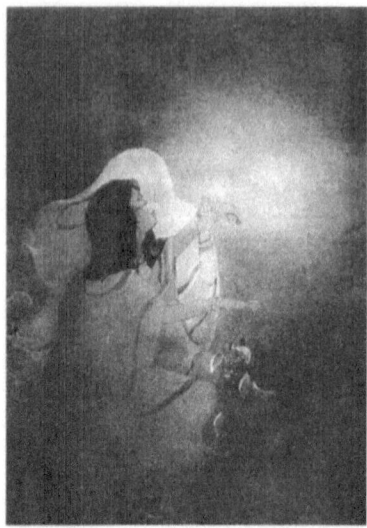

"The Finale" Rendering ideological friction. Painting by Samarendranath Gupta.

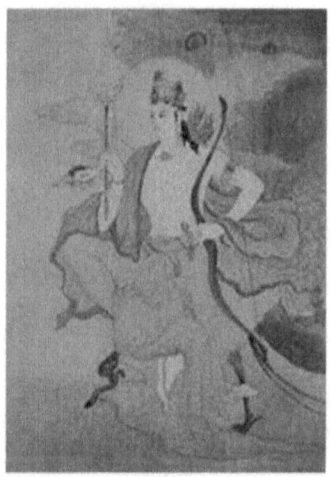

"Karthikeya" Hindu Puranic theme in wide representational use. Painting by Surendranath Ganguly.

Notes

1. *Dr. Ratan Parimoo, "Art of Three Tagores, (Abanindranath, Gaganendranath and Rabindranath) Page no. 34,*

2. *As per Journal of Indian Art, Vol.1, London, October 1883.*

3. *There were a number of exhibitions held. Great Exhibition in 1881, International Exhibition in Paris1877, Jaipore 1883, Deli 1902 and so on.*

4. *The 1851 great exhibition is referred by various writers like Bird wood, E B Havell in 'Art Administration in India' Journal of Royal Society of Arts, Vol. LVIII, London and later by Ratan Parimoo in his book, Three Tagores. Page no. 35.*

5. *Imperial Gazetter of India, the Indian Empire, Vol. IV, Administrative, Oxford, 1909: as refered by Dr. Ratan Parimoo Page no. 139, Three Tagores.*

6. *South Kensington is a district of West London which is a popular tourist destination due to its density of museums and cultural landmarks including Natural History Museum, the Science Museum, the Victoria and Albert Museum, Baden-Powell House and institutions such as the Royal Albert Hall, Imperial College London, the Royal Geographical Society, the Royal College of Art, the Royal College of Music. Here it means Royal College of Art.*

7. *The Indian business personal Sir Jamshetjee Jeejeebhoy, who offered Rs. 100000/-to East India Company in 1854 for the materialization of establishing the Art school.*

8. *Ananda K Coomaraswamy: Ananda Kentish Muthu Coomaraswamy (Tamil: Ānanda Kentiś Muthū Kumāraswāmī; (22 August 1877 – 9 September 1947) was a Ceylonese Tamil metaphysician, pioneering*

historian and philosopher of Indian art who was an early interpreter of Indian culture to the West. In particular, he is described as "the groundbreaking theorist who was largely responsible for introducing ancient Indian art to the West

9. *Royal kingdoms at Himachal Pradesh, Rajasthan, Punjab, and Muhgal encouraged Miniature traditions in India.*

10. *Gladston Solomone. The Bombay Revival of Indian Art, Bombay, 1923.*

11. *E B Havell kept himself away from India because of pressure from various sides. With acquired energy, he continued works more energetically on arrival.*

12. *Abanindranath based his Bengal School style on Miniature style of Rajsthan, Pahari and Mughal styles and Wash technique which they considered non European. Spread of his students all over India supported growth of Style of Bengal School.*

13. *Rabindranath appointed Nandalal Bose in Santiniketan when Abanindranath hesitated to leave Calcutta.*

14. *As stated by Jogesh Chandra Bagal. History of Govt. College of Art and Craft, Centenary, Calcutta College of Art and Craft, Calcutta, 1966.*

15. *E B Havell, Art Administration In India, Journal of Royal Societ of Arts, Vol. LVIII London, 1909.*

References

Selected readings only

1. *E B Havell, Indian Sculpture and Painting, London, 1908.*
2. *E B Havell, Ideals of Indian Art, London 1911.*

3. *Jogesh Chandra Bagal, History of Government College of Art and Craft, Centenary. Calcutta College of Art and Craft, Calcutta, 1966.*

4. *W. G Archer, Bazar Paiontings of Calcutta. The Style of Kalighat Painting. London, 1953.*

5. *E B Havell, Art administration in India, Journal of Royal Society of Arts, Vol. LVIII, London 1909.*

6. *Ananda K Coomaraswamy, The aims of Indian Art, Broad Campdon. 1908.*

7. *Dr. Ratan Parimoo, The Paintings of three Tagores, Abanindranath, Gaganendranath and Rabibdranath Tagore.*

8. *Jaya Appasamy, Abanindanath Tagore and the Art of His Times. Lalitkala Akademi, New Delhi.*

9. *K G Subramanyan. Moving Focus, Lalithakala Academy, and New Delhi.*

Modernization of Art Education in India with Reformatory Activities by Rabindranath Tagore

A bstract: *The family background of Tagore was economically and culturally able to accommodate and manage any sort of social situations. Rabindranath was surrounded by a crowd of people with immense creative energy and he was largely introduced and appreciated for the creative pursuits in literature. Grown with the feeling that he was not effectively gifted enough to make expression through visual art creations, he enviously witnessed his nephews challengingly involving in visual creative pursuits and getting widely appreciated. The art education system in India those days were meant only to support privileges of British colony aspirations. A group of people thoughtfully and vigorously made initiatives but they could only make marginal differences in the ongoing situations under the British power. With great ideals, Rabindranath Tagore began to establish Santiniketan since 1921 as a university. He came in contact with Western Modern Art education and realized his capabilities to express* *through visual art. He practiced western basics for his genuine expression and established modern art educational system with necessary additions of Indian basics in the university with help of geniuses in the house.*

Key words: Colonial Art, Tagore Family, Wash technique, Cubism, Expressionism, Blau Reiter, Bichitra Club, Kalabhawana.

Introduction: Rabindranath was born as the fourteenth child to Debendranath (son of Dwarakanath Tagore)[1] within the Tagore clan in 1861. Rabindranath had a lonely childhood due to his busy parents: and grew up in the charge of servants. Being the brother of thirteen elders in the family, apart from their father, Rabindranath had strong influence of his elder brothers. Among the elder brothers, Jyothirindranath, (the fifth son of Devendranath) and his wife Kadambari Devi had an affectionate relation to Rabindranath. With inborn magnetism towards literature Kadambari Devi cherished largely the literary pursuits of Rabindranath from childhood. While Jyothiridranath played the guardianship of Rabindranath meticulously Kadambari Devi supplied the emotional stimulus, caressing warmth and shade all of which supported the growth of novel personality of Rabindranath in to a creative genius.

Describing about Abanindranath and Gaganendranath may disclose affinity of Rabindranath towards painting. Both were the sons of Gunendranath Tagore, whose father was Girindranath, the brother of Debendranath (Father of Rabindranath). The family members of Girindranath showed strong inclination towards cultural activities like painting, music and theater, and held strong relations with cultural leaders of the society. He was tutored at home as Abanindranath could not adjust with ordinary schooling, with private tutors in rich, affectionate family atmosphere; he showed interest towards painting from his childhood. Later he studied and apprenticed from two English artists O Ghiladi and Charls Palmer. Italian painter O Ghiladi worked as the Vice Principal at the Calcutta School of Art since 1886. The apprenticeship might have been during 1890 around his age of 20, and lasted about six months.[2] Abanindranath learned from Charls Palmer and has also apprenticed under him. Charls palmer had been a teacher at South Kensington[3] and he taught Oil painting: rendering from Models with anatomy and taught the use of oil medium. Due to nervous behavior, Abanindranath could not appreciate the nude drawing and drawing from arranged human skull etc, still oriented with western academics realistic approaches in visual art. He learned establishing a studio with north light, painting from models and going out with easels and a huge bag with drawing materials.

With western art education he immediately changed his philosophical approach towards Indian aesthetics after watching a set of Irish paintings and another set of Persian paintings.[4] Shortly after seeking self expositions to epics and puranas he painted "Shukavisar" which had entirely different approach from his entire training in art and it was titled "Shuklavisar"[5] After the first Indian style painting, all his efforts continued to generate similar revelations and the much-admired style of Bengal School took birth. He concentrated in adapting sizes and stylistic approaches of Miniature for themes based on Indian Epics and Puranas. He invented and established a unique technique "Wash"[6]. It was followed by numerous artists known to him, his students at Calcutta school and later following his style was unavoidable for several unknown artists in nook and corners of India, which established as the Indian style painting.

Gaganendranath Tagore (brother of Abanindranath), began painting at the age of 38 in 1905 and painted more than one thousand paintings which included several mediums, and themes[7]. He started his attempts in art with landscapes done in Puri, followed by scenes from Calcutta and illustrations for My Reminiscences of Rabindranath, Chaithanya series of pictures and night series (most of them are in Black and white), caricatures and Himalayan paintings, he embarked up on a series of experiments resembling cubistic excavations of western artists- most of them in black and white or in less colors. Gaganendranath Tagore was most appreciated for his experimental works showing affinity towards cubism. The first cubistic paintings appeared in Rupam Magazine of 1922 with an article titled "An Indian Cubist" by Dr. Stella Kramrisch[8] for his experimental productions: followed by many reviewers referring the works of Gaganendranath Tagore during 1920s to cubism and post cubism.

All are aware of the fact that when Rabindranath Tagore took lifelong ample efforts to establish his literary pursuits, he tried to establish his visual creative efforts only later in life. He was surrounded with a number of artists and creative personalities during his entire life including his family verve at Jorasanko[9]. Rabindranath Tagore was enviously watching the art activities and establishments of his nephews Abanindranath and Gaganendranath, the artists established their career much before Rabindranath Tagore and made insight to establish his creative visual production as a major vocation. Rabindranath Tagore was in illusion and believed that his faith had refused him pass across the strict boundaries of letters[10]. This is an occasion in which Rabindranath explained about his own feelings towards his stagnated stage in visual expression. In several venues he was in of not able to express through visual arts.anguish. He remained assessing various occasions, found his nature not matching to the strength of response that was forceful enough to the level of his nephews.

During several occasions Rabindranath was well exposed to modern art in his later and advanced life. He was in contact with many modern artists abroad including Europe, during his visit to celebrate his Nobel Prize winning personality as a man of literature. Well known French artist Andre Karpeless was a great friend of Tagore family and arranged several art gallery visits during their visit to France. It cannot be neglected the chance of Rabindranath meeting the artists Emil Nolde, Kandinsky and Paul Klee during this visit, with help of Andre Karpeless. There is no chance to miss them while they visited Expressionist galleries and painters. One can understand how important the visit to Germany was, when one evaluates the personal growth of Rabindranath after this period. As per the Bauhaus Archive at Darmstadt, Rabindranath visited Bauhaus School at Weimer in 1921. With spent effort from Rrabindranath, exhibition of Bauhaus painters was held at Calcutta in 1922 which included the paintings of Kandinsky and Paul Klee. "This is the first time the original works of continental artists representing the latest phases of 'Post Impressionism, Post Cubism, and Expressionism have been exhibited in India. The section devoted to this class of Exhibits has been contributed by

Russian, Swiss, and German Artists."[11] O C Ganguly explains that Paul Klee exhibited his painting "Passing through an open door' in this exhibition with paintings of Russian artist Wassily Kandinsky and Johanness Itten were also exhibited in this show along with Paul Klee's. In exchange, an exhibition of Bengal School painters was planned at Berlin in the previous year. Two travelling exhibitions of similar kind had also been sent out to America. Experiences acquired through these exposures might have put ignition to his lifelong dream to be an artist of experimentation and was successful at establishing such. It might have assumed that Rabindranath had had the richest visual experience of modern painting in these visits more profound than any other Indian painter could access.

There are several theories regarding the experiments of Rabindranath after his exposure in the Indian scenario as an artist. Art historians and theoreticians took pains to explain and argue to prove presence of various elements such as rhythm, automatism, inspiration with child art, and relation of his paintings with Primitive art in the past. These cannot be neglected because, the artist was much sound person psychologically and capable of initiating things similar to the points of their arguments in comparison with facts anybody else could visualize in his paintings. It can be assessed that the visual experience and theoretical understanding he created by his visits in art destinations in Europe or elsewhere made Rabindranath bold enough to express his feelings through visual media. The understandings he made about the sense of capability is not by the abundance of skills deposited by birth in an artist but by the strength of communication a man could evoke innovatively for the desired communication at the moment he requires it. Rabindranath's activities after this stage as an artist reflect these facts to any observer. The supports of Kadambari Devi for his literary pursuits are to be remembered in this connection.

But the unsatisfied intentional mind of the poet was in search of occasion to begin to reflect his feelings through images at any moment he found suitable for the same. Even limited with ability of craft, he was wise and thoughtful enough to understand the limitations of the art practices experienced by his nephews Abanindranath and Gaganendranath when he followed the essence of Western Art. While visiting Japan years ago to his visit to Europe, Rabindranath wrote to Gaganendranathon 8th August of 1916: "Gagan, when on the earth are you going to step out of the house and travel the world? You should prove your name. But it is idle to chase you people. I have given much thought.......there is nothing as good for an awakening of consciousness as a good jolt from outside.......[12].

As continued travel in Japan, he wrote. "Aban.... The more I travel in Japan the more I feel that you should have been here, too. Squatting there all the time in your south verandhah you will never realize how very essential it is to have contact with the living art of Japan so that our own art may revive and flourish....... If you were here, the thick scales would have dropped off your eyes, the goddess of art in you would have received her true offering. It is only when I paid my visit to Japan that I realized how your art has failed to come true. But what, indeed, can I do? None of you will ever get out......."[13]

Once when he began to produce art, with greater understanding of his limitations, due to his illiteracy on it and weaknesses, he himself acknowledged on productions, Rabindranath logically argued for acceptance of his creative visual efforts. He generalized the situation in the words "All traditional structures of art must have a sufficient degree of elasticity to grow with its growth, to dance it with its rhythm".[14] Pointing the demerits of the then prevailed art education system in art schools in India, he said "I strongly urge our artists vehemently to deny their obligation carefully to produce something that can be labeled as Indian art according to some old world mannerism. Let them proudly refuse to be herded into a pen like branded beasts that are treated as cattle but not as cows."[14] After deciding the approach to be taken on his adventure of creating painting, he announced "Let us take heart and make daring experiments, venture out into the open road in the face of all risks, go through experiences in the great world of human mind, defying holy prohibitions preached by prudent little critics…."[14]

Rabindranath produced a large number of pictures with a rude powerful visual energy in them as a genuine personal signature of him, which are connected to rhythm, automatism, child art and expressionism. All his paintings followed a small format on paper, most of the time with dark colors, without or with little use of colors or tonal gradations which included beast like forms, human portraits, self portraits, tree trunks, anonymous figures and landscapes. Also the pictures had a kind of theatricality and always the figure appeared in its surface like the appearance of an actor on stage.

With ambition to establish as an artist of caliber, Rabindranath Tagore was curiously witnessing his surroundings. When he saw the trends prevailed in the western countries, he understood the lack of our artists, laying low down in acceptance of traditions, usages and establishments. Artists kept themselves in its invisible but psychological bounding; they were lost themselves, and deficiently deposited as incompetent to make any breakthrough in art practice which made Rabindranath thoughtful and arrogant.

The well known literary figure and friend of Tagore, Victoria Occampo to whom the Purabi manuscripts were dedicated described later about her experience of watching erasures are said to be the first known attempts to Rabindranath to visualize art forms. " making lines that suddenly jumped into life out of this play: prehistoric monsters, birds, faces appeared"[15]. Beginning with these images Rabindranath Tagore came into the lime light for more than a decade for his role of experimental visual art production till his death in 1941.

Rabindranath was very much vigilant about the art situations developed by his nephews. Abanindranath Tagore was in association with Ananda K Coomaraswamy and E B Havell as well as many others geniuses of his life time, both were promoters of changes in all cultural establishments of their time. E B Havell was British appointed superintend for the art institution in Calcutta during this period. He tried to awaken art education system with the help of several Indian people but Havell had to leave his initiatives due to the loss of positions from British colonial Government. It was hardly possible to find any interest of Rabindranath in the development of ideologically Indian connected aesthetic creation by the group of artists in Calcutta and in the establishment of the Bengal School. One could only see a passive viewer in Rabindranath during Bengal School activities and criticize later when exposed to world art. It is assumed that his stagnation was due to being kept himself away from possibilities of visual art with acknowledgements on own illiteracy on visual terms.

In 1901 the multifarious genius Rabindranath Tagore established a co-educational school inside the premises of the Brahmacharya Ashram established by his father Debendranath Tagore in the land in a far away village of West Bengal which has received from Zamindars of Raipur in 1863. By arranging continuous programs like Hindu *melaas* every year in this venue by Tagore, it become a centre of nationalist activity in every sense. Rabindranath Tagore believed in open air education and had reservations about any teaching done within four walls due to his belief that walls represent conditioning of mind. Matching with Gandhi, Tagore did not have a good opinion about the western method of education introduced by the British in India. Tagore once said, "I do not remember what I was taught, I only remember what I learnt". Following to Tagore's idea on education "every person is genius and that all students may not bloom at the same time"[16] a new system of learning was devised in Visva-Bharati. Tagore visualized his university as a 'seat of learning' where courses are planned according to the demand of the student/s and education continued until both the student and the teacher got satisfied. On receipt of this ideological thread, Gandhi and Nehru played important roles and supported in its appropriation as a Central University in 1951.

The students engaged in games as well in production of useful objectivities, including conduct of night schools in villages. "In the educational program emphasis is given to Music and Art, for it is clearly recognized that the great use of education is not merely to collect facts, but to know man and make oneself known to man. Every student is expected to learn, at least to some extent, not only the language of intellect, but also the language of art- to obtain a mastery of lines and colors, sounds and movements."[16] According to the notes in Viswabharati Quarterly, various schools were established including Purva Vibhaga (Santiniketan School), Kala Bhavan (School of Arts and Crafts), Narivibhaga (Ladies College), Krishi Vibhaga (Department of Agriculture and Rural Reconstruction) and Uttara Vibhaga (Visva Bharati College) aiming unique special studies in them in Visva Bharati. Among the schools Kala Bhavan was a school of painting with distinctive features of its own said to be under the supervision of Abanindranath Tagore who was the director. A school of music was also developed in its own lines. Choral singing was practiced as well as individual voice production. Attention was given to classical instrumental music and the services of eminent musicians were secured for special courses from time to time. In the crafts section practical training was given in fresco painting, lacquer work, book binding, terracotta etc. under the supervision of qualified teachers and indigenous craftsmen. There was a small museum attached to those departments also a library also which aims at bringing together materials for a comparative study of the different systems of music and different schools of art which lay scattered in the different provinces of India, and in the different strata of society, and also those belonging to the other great countries of Asia, which had communications with India.

Abanindranath, his brother Gaganendranath, Dr. Ananda K Coomaraswamy, Sister Niveditha, Ganen Maharaj, Mahendranath Dutta, Okakura Kakuzo, J C Bose, Girish Chandra Ghosh, Satheesh Chandra Mukherjee, Rabin Narayan Ghosh, Akshayakumar Maitra, Sir John Woodroffe, Lord Carmichael, Lord Ronaldshay, Miss Macleod were some people surrounded in Bengal due to various cultural reasons who witnessed all these activities. In 1909 Lady Herringham[17] sought advice of Sister Nivedita and Abanindranath Tagore to take assistance of young energetic Nandalal Bose along with Asit Kumar Haldar, Samarendranatha Gupta and Venkattappa to create fresh copies of paintings in Ajanta where Ganen Maharaj was looking after their wellness. Since then Nandalal worked at Jorasanko House and the friendship with Rabindranath increased by helping with illustrations of his books. Even the matter was in mind of Rabindranath Tagore for long time; only in 1914 Rabindranath welcomed Nandalal Bose to Santiniketan where he found his own friends Asitkumar Haldar and Mukul Dey who were already working.

In 1916, Bichitra club[18] was organized by Rabindranath Tagore at his residence at Calcutta along with his nephews Abanindranath, Gaganendranath, and so many others. It comprised poetry reading, staging of plays, organized musical programs, debates issues on art, music, literature, social issues and started modest art activity programs. Nandalal Bose, Asitkumar Haldar, Surendranath Kar and Mukul Dey were founder members of it and N K Dayal the only sculptor with them. Arai Kampo the Japanese painter in relation with Okakura Kakuzo who was in India by invitation of Rabindranath, at the time, tried a cultural exchange with Indian painting and Japanese ink painting technique. Nandalal took advantage of this occasion with keen interest in Japanese technique. Vichitra could not go much further due to departure of teachers due to various reasons. Finally in July 1917, Surendranath moved to Santiniketan on the request of Rabindranath because Nandalal could not make his mind.

Conclusion: Nandalal was interested to go to Santniketan since his first visit but only after his wandering and working in various places, in July 1919, Nandalal started working at Kala Bhawana, the art department of Visva Bharati. In between he was asked by Abanindranath Tagore to work with Calcutta school but finally he decided to work with Santiniketan. Under his teaching methodology, the teaching system of Santiniketan flourished for thirty five years. It is very important to note the faculty members including Indian and foreigner brought up the institution to its well organized pattern, Nandalal Bose, Andre Carpeles (French painter and Craft women), Liza Von Pott (Viennese Scultpress), Mrs. Milward (British Sculptress pupil of bourdelle) and Dr. Stella Kramrisch (Austrian Art Historian, student of Prof. Strygovsky.) The students were introduced in western aesthetics as well as Indian. Many artists well known in the modern Indian art will acknowledged their debt to these indigenous teachers whether they are directly connected with the initial movement or not: for example Ramendranath Chakravarti and Mukul Dey in Calcutta, Ahivasi in Bombay, Ravishankar Raval and Somalal Shah in Gujarat, Samarendranath Gupta Rupkrishna in Lahore and D P Roy Chowdhury in Madras. When all the other faculty members supported the growth of the institution with their practical knowledge, Dr. Stella Kramrisch made it with her theoretical wisdom on art. So that with the inspirations received from Bauhaus school set up in Germany some years ago, Rabindranath built a new art institution ideologically the most modern in India which continues its outstanding performance so far. But establishing an institution does not mean too much for satisfying ideological demands of the poetic genius. He continued his searches with demands initiated from genuine thirsts for the same.

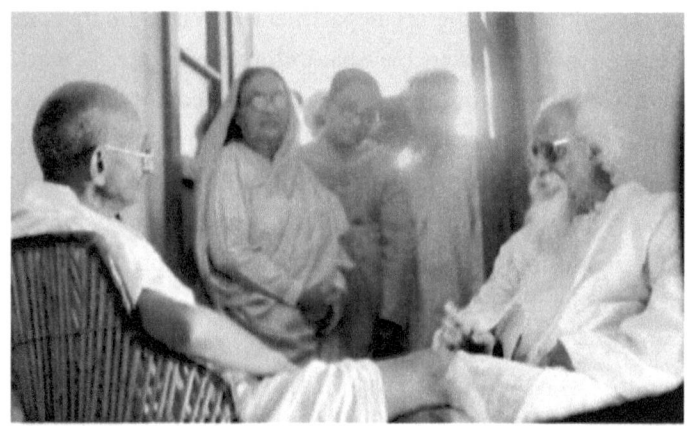

Rabindranath Tagore with Mahatma Gandhi.

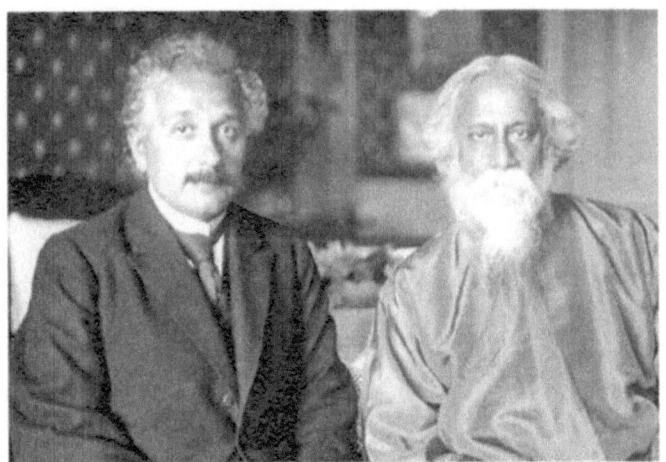

Rabindranath Tagore with Albert Einstein

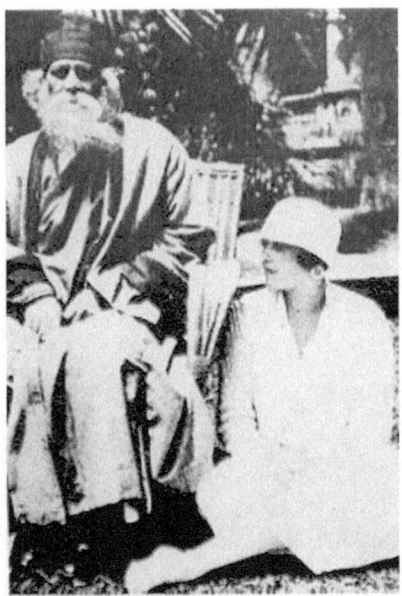

RabindranathTagore with Victoria Occampo.

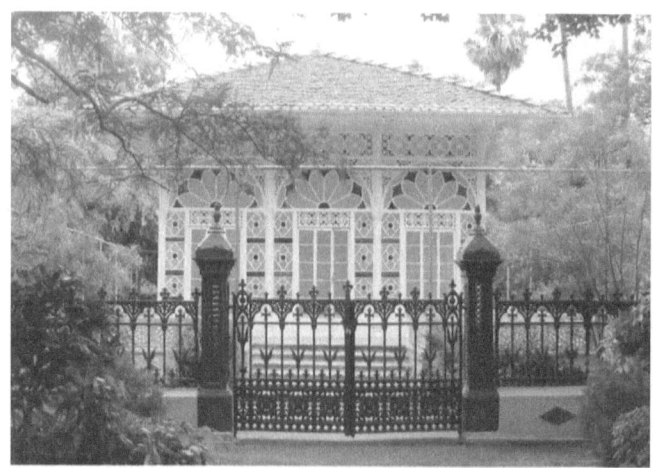

The Asram built by Father of Rabindranath at Santiniketan for Meditation.

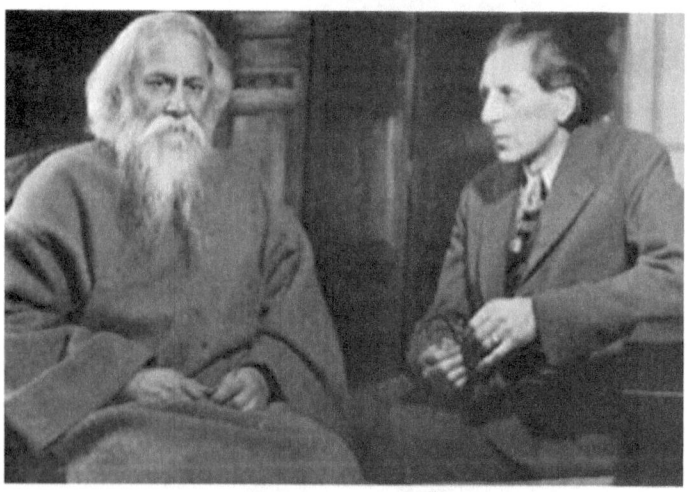

Rabindranath Tagore with Ananda Kentish Coomaraswamy.

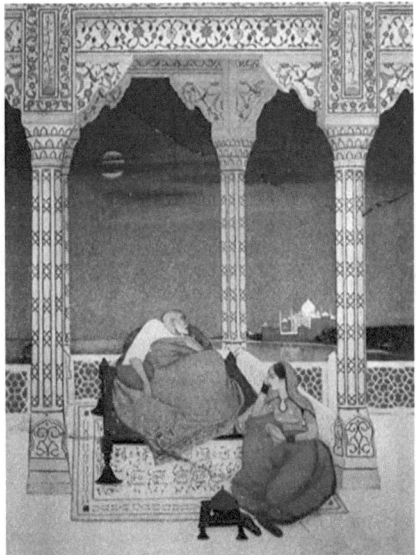

A painting by Artist Abanindranath Tagore.

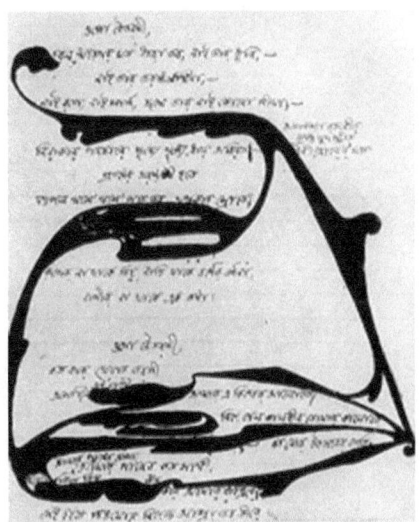

One of the first erasures by Artist Rabindranath Tagore in Purabi manuscript.

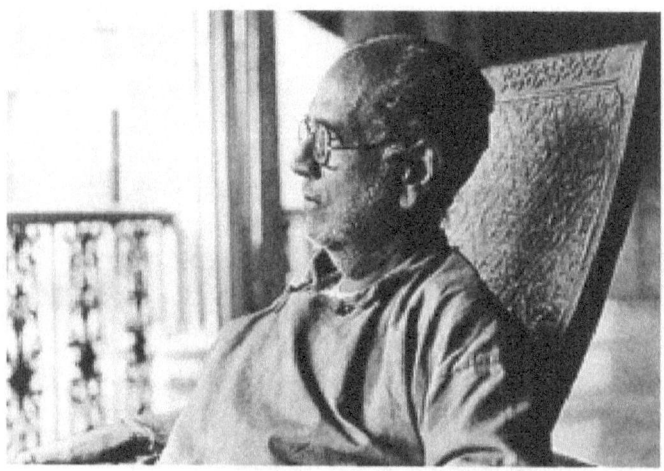

Artist Abanindranath Tagore.

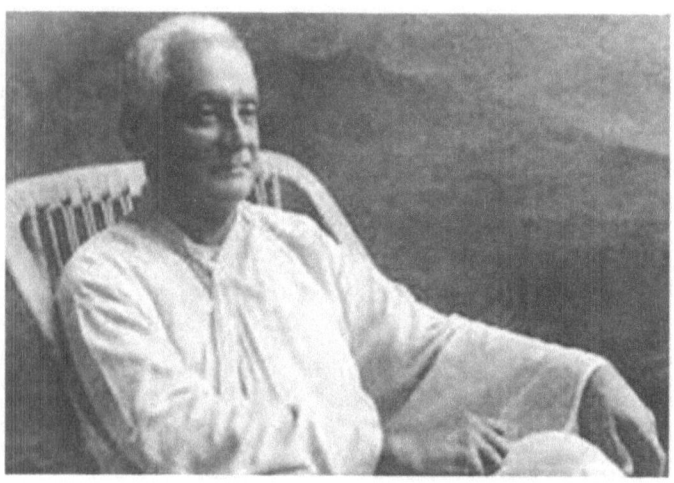

Artist Gaganendranath Tagore.

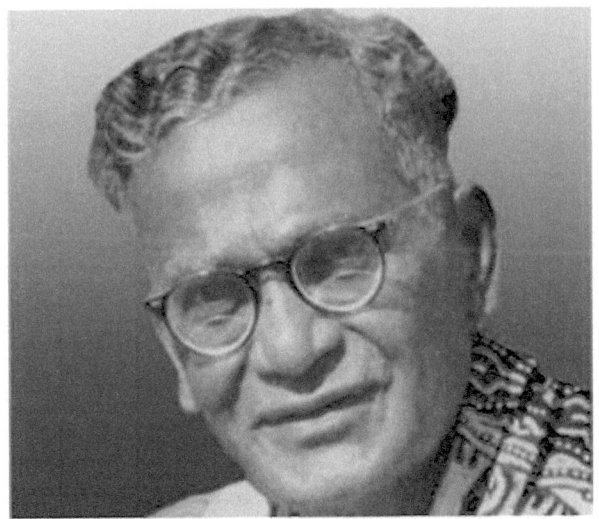

Artist Nandalal Bose.

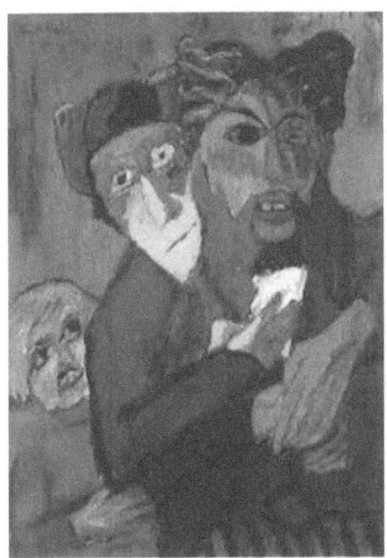

Painting of Artist Emil Nolde.

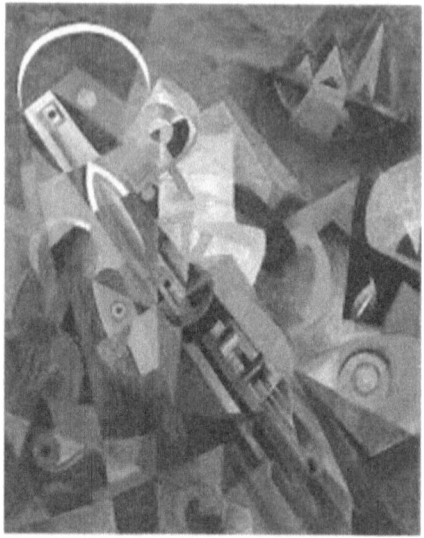

Painting of Artist Johannas Itten.

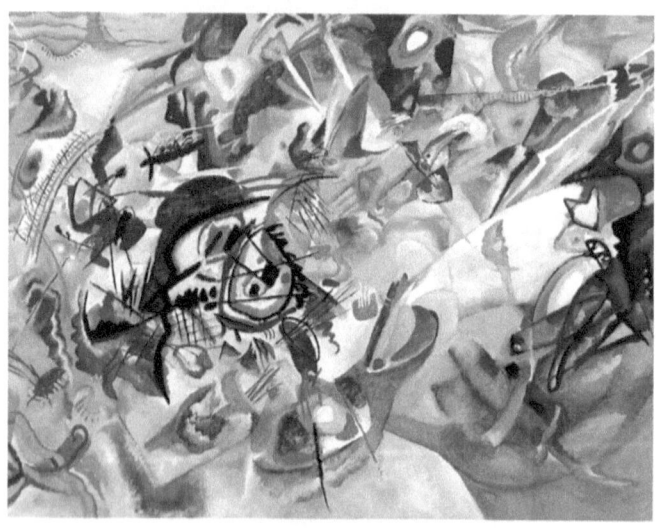

Painting by Artist Wassily Kandinsky.

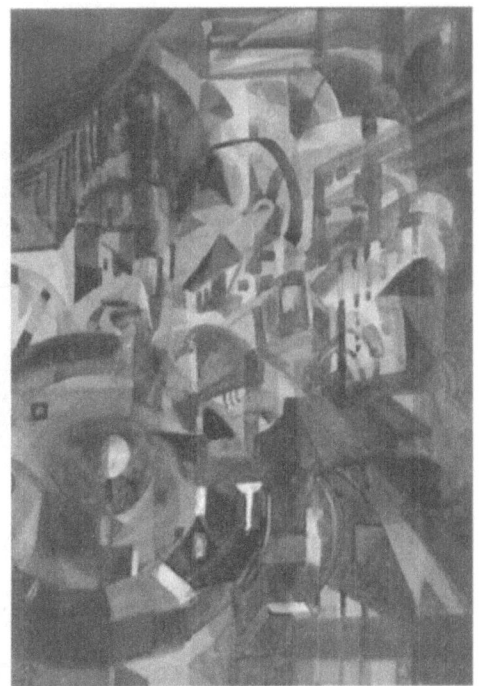

Painting by Artist Gaganendranath Tagore.

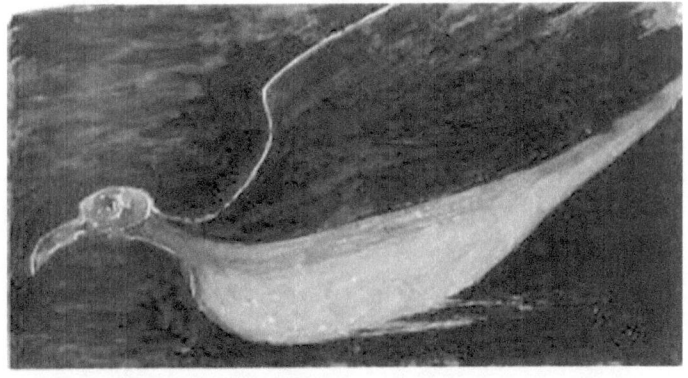

Bird, Painting by Artist Rabindranath Tagore.

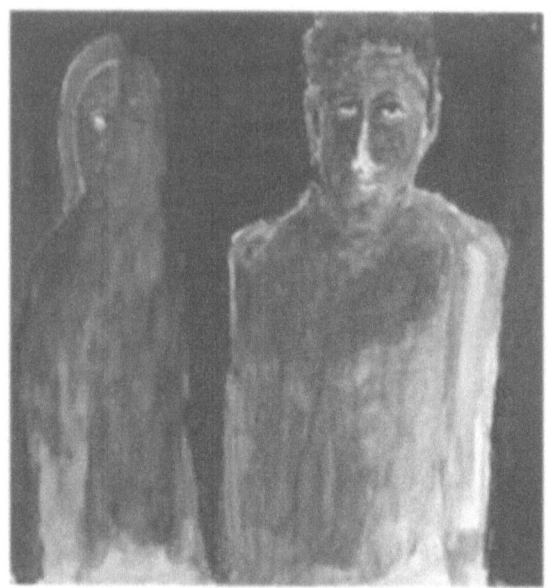

Women and Man, painting by Artisty Rabindranath Tagore.

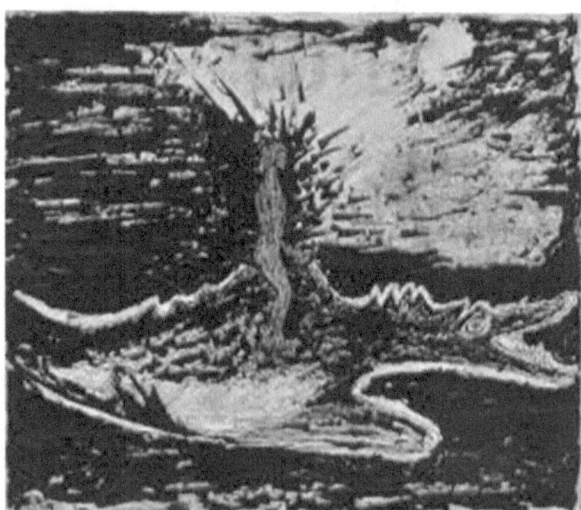

The Crocodile, by Artist Rabindranath Tagore.

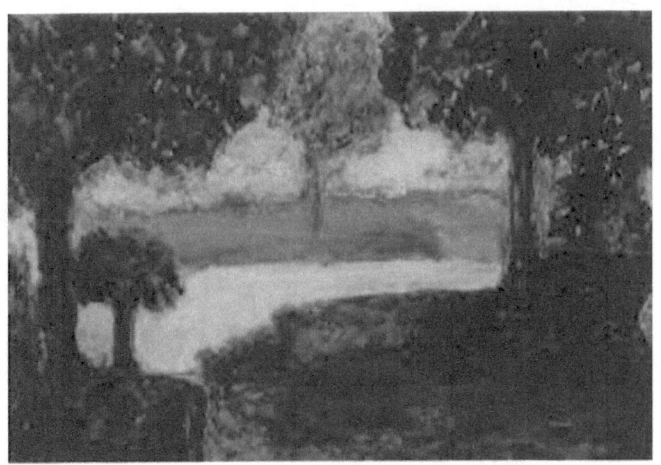

A Landscape by Artist Rabindranath Tagore.

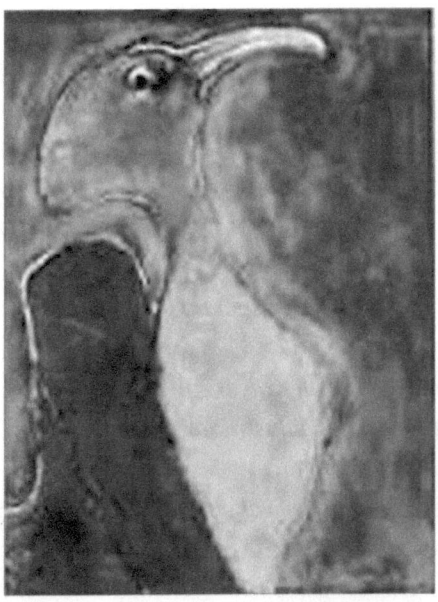

Again a bird, Painting by Artist Rabindranath Tagore.

Notes

1. *Rabindranath Tagore. Rabindranayth's father Debendranath was the eldest son of Debendranath Tagore the founder of Tagore clan we generally discuss.*

2. *Dr. Rattan Parimoo. "The Paintings of Three Tagores-Abanindranath, Gaganendranath and Rabindranath Page 73.*

3. *South Kensington: Area belongs to current Royal College of Art and surroundings.*

4. *The Irish pictures received from English lady and the Miniature painting with Persian influence he saw gave him insight of the painters' role.*

5. *First Indian style painting of Abanindranath Tagore. 'Shuklabisar' is a painting following miniature format shows a women dressed in white sari is waiting her lover in a forest area. The lower portion of the painting is decoratively calligraphed in Bengali and boundaries are drawn with curly margin lines decoratively. It is like a manuscript Illustration of the period.*

6. *Wash is the technique of water based medium on paper innovated and initiated by Abanindranath Tagore in which the artist dip the painting in water and dry several times for perfection and hazy effects.*

7. *Various themes of Gaganendranath- Puri Landscapes, Portrait sketches, illustrations for My Reminiscences of Rabindranath Tagore.*

8. *Dr. Stella Kramrisch was an Austrian Art historian invited by Rabindranath for seeking guidance in Art education and its Theoretical teaching, a unique approach in India, the poet experimented from his Bauhaus learning. She*

was a student of Prof. Strygovsky who was familiar to poet.

9. *Jorasanko House. The family mansion of the Jorasanko quarter of Calcutta.*

10. *Nephews of Rabindranath Tagore. Check the Note-1 for detail.*

11. *O C Ganguly, The New Art In Europe, ViswaBharati Quarterly Vol-1, April 1923, no-1, Article from page number 69 to75*

12. *The letter dated 8th August of Rabindranath is quoted by Ashok Mitra in the forces behind the Modern Movement, Lalitkala Contemporary No.1, June 1962, New Delhi.*

13. *As quoted by RatanParimoo, "Paintings of Three Tagores, Abanindranath, Gaganendranath and Rabindranath", Page 115. Pub. M S university Baroda.*

14. *Quoted Tagore's own words. Tagore in Art and tradition, on Art and Aesthetics 1921.*

15. *Victoria Occampo, Tagore on Banks of the River Plate: A centenary Volume, SahityaAkademi. New Delhi Page 196.*

16. *Rabindranath Tagore. VisvaBharati Quarterly Journal, Vol-1. On April 1923.(Vishakha 1330)*

17. *During the winter of 1909, the British artist Lady Herringham copied murals of Ajanta with the help of a team of artists including Nandalal Bose, Samarendranatha Gupta, Asit Kumar Haldar and Venkettappa.*

18. *Bichitra club; An ideological teaching place for art were begun at Jorasanko house of Tagores from 1915 with which all artists like Nandalal Bose, A. K. Haldar, Suren Kar, N K Deval, MukulDey were all worked and Gaganendranath*

established his Graphics studio for making Prints. It was closed after establishment of Santiniketan.

References

Selected Readings only

1. *Mulk Raj Anand, Birth of Lalit Kala, Lalitkala Contemporary-1, LalitkalaAkademi, ND. Page 3-7.*
2. *Mulk Raj Anand, The four Initiators of the ContemporaryExperimentalism, Lalitkala Contemporary-2, LalitkalaAkademi, Page 1-5. Pub 1962.*
3. *The Modern movement of art in India, A symposium, Lalitkala Contemporary-1, Page8-38.*
4. *W. G Archer, "India and Modern Art Ruskin House, George Allen &Unvin Ltd. Museum Street London. Pages 144.*
5. *K G Subramanyan, "The Living Tradition", A Classic collection, Seagull Books, Calcutta, 1987.*
6. *The VisvaBharati Quarterly, Volume 49, Numbers 1-4, May 1983-April 1984. Nandalal Centenary Number. VisvaBharati, Santiniketan. Pages 262.*
7. *Papers read in the Abanindra Centenary Seminar, Organized by the Department of History of Art, Kala bhavana, Visvabahrati, February-1973. Abanindranath Pub. By. Abanindra Centenary Celebration Committee, Visvabharati.Pub.*
8. *Sisirkumar Ghosh Ed. Some writings of Nandalalbose, A viswabharatiBooklet. Reprinted from Visvabharati Quarterly Volume 34.*
9. *Jogesh Chandra Bagal, Government College of Art & Craft Calcutta, School of Industrial Art 1854, Govt.*

School of Art 1865, Govt. College of Art& craft 1951. Pages 90.

10. *Rabindranath Tagore. Ed. The VisvaBharati Quarterly. Vol.1, April 1923. No.1*

11. *Dr. Ratanparimoo. "The Paintings of the Three Tagores, Abanindranath, Gaganendranath, Rabindranath", Pub. M S university, Baroda.*

Various Critical Factors Required Care for Maintenance of Modernization on Art Education in India

A bstract: *Modernization process that took place on Art Education in India was a continuation of similar processes that took place in various venues all over the world, beginning from the Florentine School which supported many major artists like Michelangelo. There is a straight clear path definable from 15th century developments through Salon de Refuses in Paris, and establishments of various schools all over the World to modern developments in India. In India British promoted art production in the lines of their tastes and educated Indian Artists productions to suits their tastes. In the past there was several developments that led to the promotion of an art education system which has roots with Bauhaus school of Europe. Starting from initiation of Kalabhavana by Tagore, we also fell in to the line of progress. It requires special care to keep the attitude of modernization while evaluating all different affecting faculties including changes in our walks of lives.*

Key words: Modernization, Florence School, Salon de Refuses, Luvre, Bauhaus, Colonial Period, E B Havell, Tagore, Stella Karmrisch, N S Bendre, College of Fine Arts, Cholamandalam, Aesthetics.

Introduction: Application of a systematic approach on Art Education was began to be followed since establishment of the Florentine school. Intellectual products of this school like Da Vin ci, Michelangelo, Giorgio Vasari[1] and many others proved their efficiency in painting, sculpture and architecture by 15th century, by getting commissions from Medici family, the ever gigantic supports to cultural developments in history. Apart from individual activities of artists, they altogether made a productive teaching to the world around and in a later period it gathered a global cultural acknowledgement when the communication means developed into various levels. The artists worked in similar understandings (like mannerists) shaped inimitable style of teachings to the society where they dwelled in. There are several isms followed by and each of them marked evidence of its potentials during their existence in its time and space.

With challenging movements against French Royal society on its quality analysis by jury for selection to annual exhibition, the artists stepped on to a new mode at art practice. The protest against Salon[2] and silent acceptance of the Royal, Napoleon III, took profile as a new teaching towards reception to public opinion. The effect by existence and continuation of Luvre Museum as a visual acknowledgement and proof for developments in art of past and its changing ethics over past several centuries is an outstanding success over all uncertainties in this connection.

The art tendencies took shape after these incidents were totally beyond tendencies on art prevailed in Europe and any other part of the globe. However all these tendencies took its own special role in teaching the public, about viewpoints on production and management of art objectivities in the manner they thought their right.

Bauhaus school[3] initiative by Walter Gropius, Moholly Nagy, Paul Klee and many creative geniuses like Kandinsky made unparallel establishments in human mind by its activities a century ago. With the advent of Hitler and Nazi activists the Bauhaus spread to various parts of the globe and continued its growth to where ever they made escape in the globe. With all these changes through several centuries art education adapted a kind of standardization by exchange of ideas with the space and time where ever it welcomed openly. The standardization accepted inclusion of art historical studies and philosophical studies on art, studies from natural sources, studies of human anatomy, and other living organisms, acknowledgement of perspective and volume, innovative attempts in new mediums, adaptation of new thought processes, tendencies of experimentations and so on.

In India, the first avenue for the acceptance of Bauhaus school tendencies was Kalabhawana of Santiniketan, at the new school began by poet Rabindranath Tagore. Dr Stella Kramrisch[4] was introduced to teach art historical revelations to its beneficiaries at Kalabhawana. It was an experimental activity but followed by the introduction of many art historians like Charls Fabri[5]. The teaching style of the school changed immensely soon and it established a standardized system of art teaching against colonial art schools and ideological conventions propagated by them. The schools started by British during their rule in various upcoming cites in India were basically for the support of their wishes and ideologies, but the genius engagements like the one made by E B Havell[6] at Calcutta colonial school, challenged conventional British ideologies, and soon the art education scenario in each venue was shifted to a new one, which has strong affiliation with emerging tendencies on science, technology, trade, politics, ideological synthesis and social requirements. The major focal point here to be noted is the standardization of art education system in the background of a completely traditional society, adjusting with various tendencies of the emerging world and acceptance of its necessity in the current society.

Investigating current status: The teaching style of Santiniketan was initially set up by Nandalal Bose and it was followed by several artists like Benode Behari Mukherjee, Ram Kinker Baij and K G Subramanyan,[7] all of who have acquired recognition as art teachers and celebrated art professionals. The education system followed in Santiniketan was able to provide a door of art professionalism wide open to its beneficiaries. It is important to note that establishment of this school was against to the then existing art schools including the one in Madras led by D P Roy Chowdhuri[8]. When teaching and results associated matters are on focus, an evaluator can feel absence of an art teacher on the retirement of D P Roy Choudhury, until his student K C S Paniker[9] came in to teaching position at Madras School. It might have critically viewed when the art schools in upcoming cities in India were largely supported by British colonial system during their govern ship.

During the inception of Faculty of Fine Arts at Maharaja Sayajirao University, the administrator Markhandeya Bhatt and Painter Prof. N S Bendre[10] made efforts for the creation of an outstanding art educational atmosphere there. The faculty there persistently worked on its smooth and authorized status. It is to be measured that, apart from Santiniketan, the only art institution equally measured by artists for its potential of professionalism is the institution at Baroda as both had vital inputs of marked genius personalities from the dates of beginning.

Simultaneously the professionalism celebrated by various art groups like Bombay Progressive Art Group, Calcutta Group, Progressive Artist's Association in Madras, Shilpi Chakra at New Delhi and Group 1890 made an awakening on art activities all over the cityscapes of India.[11] When art was accepted in the society as equal to any other subject factor such like Sciences, Social Sciences, Engineering, Historical studies and any other branch of studies, the demand for art institutions increased and several art schools began to function all over India. It began to be considered as an essential integral part of university education in India. It is also noted that the artist's enthusiasm to learn art abroad, made them seek suitable up gradation of abilities utilizable for the modernization process.

The current art education style materialized through modernization in several venues through a large time span. Currently we could see that the teaching of art has been considered as a major subject and objectivity in universities and art educational institutions with understandings of equality to any other subject. A disciple can select any one of the branches from several specializations and opt for higher education. The under graduate degree studies on art begin with common studies of all subjects for one or two years and continuation of studies of specialization subject for three years. Further studies bestow the student's chances for specialization of any one of the subjects for two years in postgraduate level. In advanced institutions the subjects are specifically taught and their courses are planned for more effective involvement to the subject chosen for specialization by the student. As the education generally came into platform to look for research based understandings, subject based specializations and specifications came into more potential existence and studying all different modes in post graduate level unproductively turned meaningless. The efforts of University Grants commission to focus and centralize the art education system with equal standards of general education are also mentionable here.

Theoretical studies which include the studies on History of Art and Philosophy of Art are unavoidable elements of art education and professional practice. When the theoretical studies have its special role on art practice, it has certain limitations such as the difference between visual art and literary contributions have different grooming and functional entities. Since art production is a psychological phenomenon (feeling)[12] connected with potential ability to create (connected to craft), when the quantity of literary understanding increases the stagnation of the artistic process increases. As the rate of literally elaborative nature decreases in a work of art, the aesthetic flattering of the objectivity taken places.

Since its inception the efforts made by Central Lalit Kala Akademi, New Delhi is a major factor of influence in coordination of "Beingness as artist", the feeling of an Indian

National. The Triennalle India (International Exhibitions) brought a sort of internationalization in artists and venues related with it. Art, mortality as an artist and his longing as an artist were the ideologies of various artists groups that began to function but the artists group at Chennai made its most initiative step by gathering of artists in their own Artists Village in Cholamandalam. It permanently marked its ideological necessity for the thoughtful survival further as artists. Jahangir Art Gallery in Mumbai, established a professionalism of art and its marketing which exposed potentials of gallery system in India, to a venue exposed to Metro cityscape. Currently there are thousands of Art Galleries successfully doing business each day favoring art and artists which reminds a "Global Totter"[13]. The Indian situations are booming equal to any International business venue in the West, where art was socially accepted largely in much advance due to various related factors.

Modernization of any objectivity is not always accidental. We have now learned to put into practice planned changes and reformations aiming modernization. The process of implementation normally begins with prepared work outs for the employment of acquired knowledge, through plans made for modernization. All efforts of Modernization are formulated on the basis of existing circumstances. Slowly it takes a revolution to a form that is useful for the demands of changing world. Since it has implementation status as per demands of the society, it is required to make exigent changes based on selected realities of human lives. When it is connected with lives, the approaches of "Giorgio Vasari", the Florentine artist who studied "Lives" of artists during 15th Century is absolutely justified[14].

As I pointed above, our imaginations always take growth into existing realities of time, from the perspective we look at it. Human generations are always on exploration of life realities according to rational changes in social spheres. Outcomes of all unique novel expeditions of the past get lost when it arrives at meaning of existence (modernization) in current social situations and again remain ordinary. As the nature of (existence of) modernization is questionable as such, it is very much required to sharpen the process of modernization. It is unavoidable for the creator advancement to depend on currently existing social factors in front of him. It is also required by him to evaluate all different spheres of human generations equally, during all marked time periods, comprehensively witnessed by social transcending observatories or goals.

A change which currently takes our immediate attention is the expansion and persistence of computers and its astuteness in all spheres of human life. It has already established appearance and affections in lives of human generations. The scientists have developed wide cyber space between the sparks created in minute electronic circuits. It opens to any human a gigantic world of possibilities. Various kinds of computer programs are available for connecting human activities and thought processes with mechanical devices. The manufacturers introduce mechanisms and devices suitable for any demands of the artist for expression. There is only one demerit here to note is that, the receptor of these new electronic experiments are limited by the only possibilities of the device or mechanism the receptor owns. Not creativity but the quality of mechanism the receptor owns influences the freedom of expression. The amount of appreciation and depreciation depends up on the typical occasion in which the creator immerses.

The speed of computer supported mechanisms contributes to the entire time span of creation, when the creator depends on the possibilities of it. But when the creator gets limited by the inabilities of mechanisms to render the particular and unique requirements with stamps of personality owned by him, the computer becomes futile. It is found necessary to clarify here that any of the above described here is not to measure or evaluate the abilities of programs established and locked within existing device management, by the use of binary systems in minute scrupulous electronic circuits. The mechanisms never permit any experimental activity of the creator beyond the capabilities of the programs filled within its cyber space. Any activity through mechanisms is channelized through already established parameters only. In this way the onlooker can evaluate the sound of the limitations of cyber space for the creation of uniqueness and individuality.

How the work through a mechanism can be utilized for expression of uniqueness and personality is a question of depth. New pathways are to be established for solving these issues. New methodologies are to be planned and implemented for unique utility demanded by individual creators for self expression. It is mandatory establishing creator's personality and maintaining uniqueness in any production for announcing originality. It necessary to manufacture cyber space strata filled with abilities to preconceive personal and unique requirements of the creator who proposes to utilize the mechanism. It should be capable and helps act for the creator rendering imagination accurately. It is necessary to develop such electronic circuits to be able to undertake and materialize the above requirements.

To make the creator ready with the capabilities for management and maintenance of the above status, endowment of the artists and art school students with advanced computer learning is mandatory. Computer studies should be limited to the ones who requires it and it must be limited up to level of requirement. It is a simple fact that computer can be considered only as a tool of creator like a brush or pencil but surely not the brain.

Conclusion: It is indispensable to invite attention of all the ones who care to certain most important factors before concluding. The society currently exhibits three or more strategically different situations in the art education system. When the major side of the system is equipped with abilities to confront and adjust to use for various utilities, the traditional teaching systems are lacking innovations, and are completely neglected. Contradictorily the situations, where the fake pretends like authentic in traditional knowledge and mislead the society with wrong monitory intentions, are eventually staged. So that the general public is getting confused, regarding the path to pursue and the final destination where to reach for the appreciation of aesthetics. The third notable factor is the growth of technical aspects in a commercial atmosphere, mechanization of the world day by day and thriving of individuality, uniqueness and originality against disquieting societal issues. When the one construe for maintenance of the process of modernization of Art Education in India, all various aspects discussed above are to be taken into consideration.

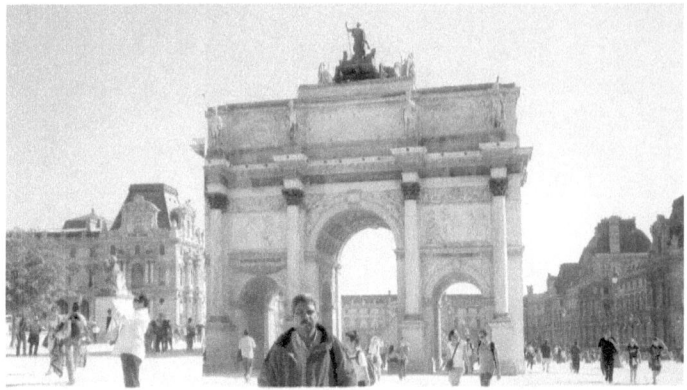

At front gate of Luvre Museum, Paris, France. This was the residential Royal Palace of Nappolean III, until he opened it with large collection of works o Art in 1860s. Currently one of the largest museums of rare acquisitions with titles never found elsewhere in the universe.

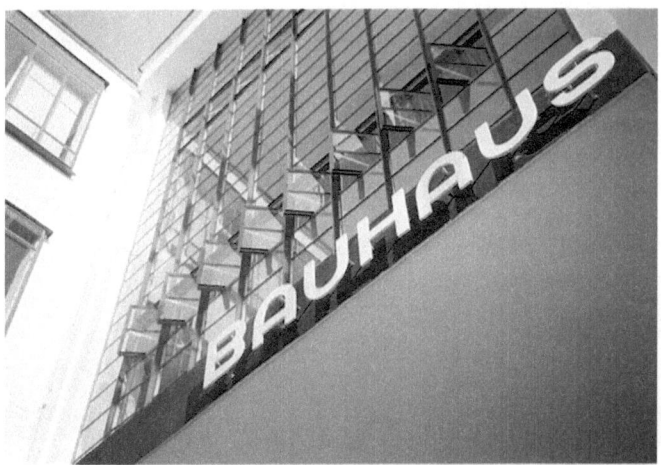

The front title sign board of "Bauhaus" School workshop at Desseau, Germany.

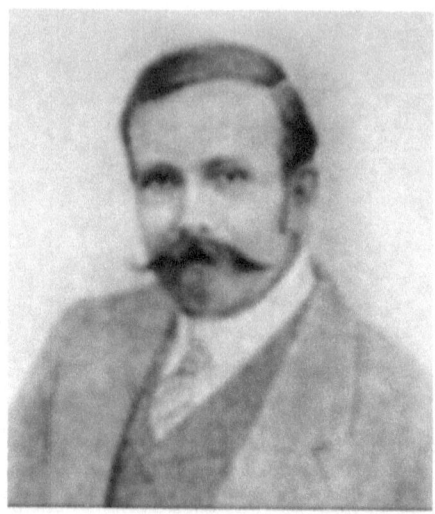

E B Havell. The superindant of Art Education School at Calcutta who sold of old British models and samples and tried for a revolution in art by bringing Indian style with help of Ananda Cooaraswami and Abanindranath Tagore. A technically produced image with use of photography vastly available.

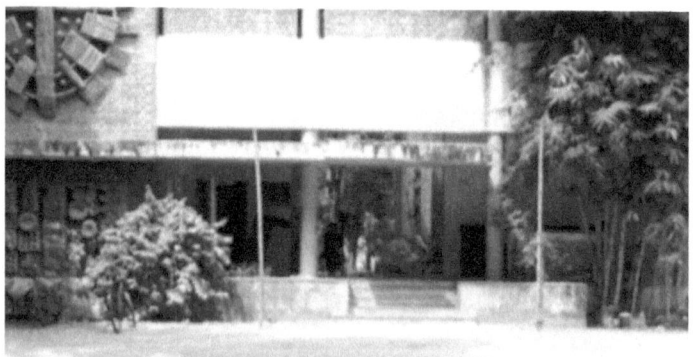

At front gate of Department of Painting, Faculty of Fine Arts, M S University, Baroda. Muhammed Shafi Photography.

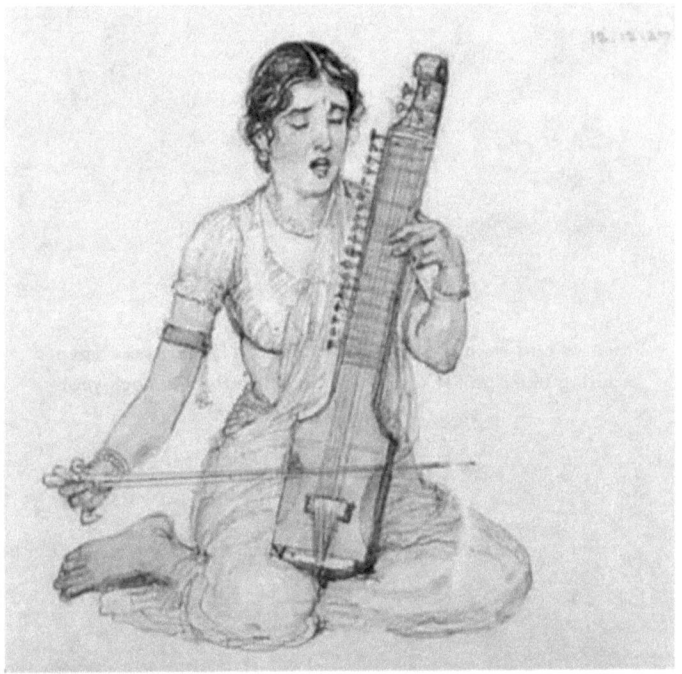

Partially colored Drawing by M V Duranhdar, done in 1927. Showing ideological confusion.

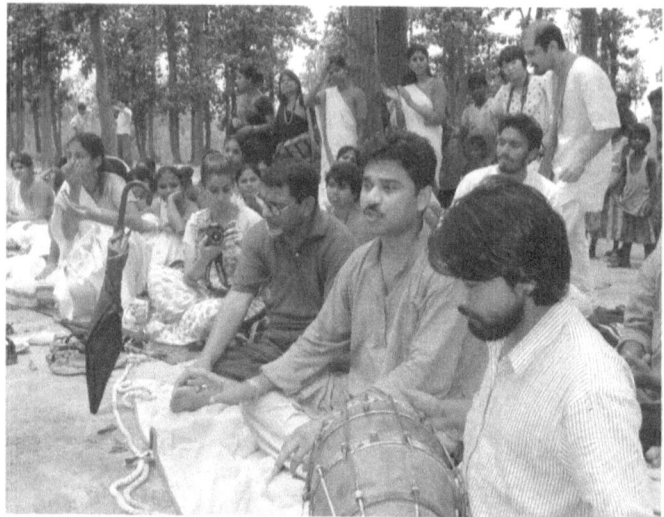

Students and Faculties on Interaction with local people opened during Nandan Mela of Viswbharati University each year.

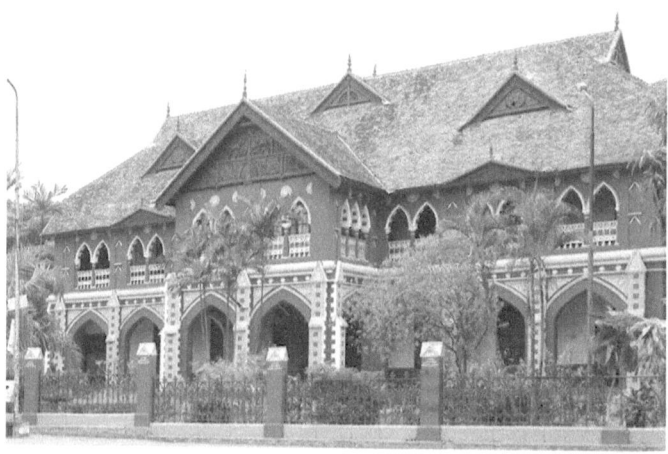

Main Academic block of College of Fine Arts, Trivandrum, Kerala. A building renovated from outline of Colonial period.

Notes

1. *Florentine School; began to establish by the end of 15th Century in Italy. Leonardo Da Vinci, Michelangello and Giorgio Vasari were products of this school and most of them were commissioned by Medici Family later.*

2. *Paris Salon: Salon began to exhibit paintings 1n early 1860s annually in Paris with the support of Napoleon III.*

3. *Bauhaus School was initaiated by Walter Groupius in association with Moholy Naggy, Paul Klee and several artists and genius like Kandinsky before 1st World War but it was closed by Nazy Govvernment during World War II.*

4. *Dr. Stella Kramrisch was invited by Rabindranath Tagore to teach Art History in Santiniketan which turned makeable in the History.*

5. *Charls Fabri could not continue in Santiniketan for long as students objected the entrance into studios with shoes. They compelled him and made him out of classrooms.*

6. *E B Havell was appointed to be the Head of the Art Institution at Calcutta. He replaced all western models with Indian style including Miniature in Calcutta School with help of Tagore brothers.*

7. *Benode Behari Mukherjee, Ramkinker Baij, and K G Subramanyan were students of Nandalal Bose, the Bengal School artist who taught in Kalabhavana.*

8. *Well known artist/ sculptor D P Roy Chowdhury was the superiendant at Madras School while KCS Paniker was a student there.*

9. *K C S Paniker become superintend of Madras School after his studies there under D P Roy Chowdhury. Later he initiated for Cholamandhalam Artists Village with his friends.*

10. *N S Bendre was Faculty in Fine Arts Faculty who introduced courses in Fine Arts there.*

11. *The Groups established in various cities, Bombay, Calcutta, Delhi, Chennai were known as Progresive Artists Groups.*

12. *Psychological Phenomenon: creativity is due to some psychological problem of the beholder. Over enthusiasm on theoretical studies an easily burden the artists and make his mind stagnated.*

13. *Global Totter, is a person travel through the various major cities of the world.*

14. *Check note 1.*

References

Selected Reading

1. *Roy C Craven, "Indian Art: A Concise History of Art". Published in 1976 by Thames and Hudson LTD, 252pages.*

2. *Benjamin Rowland, "The Pelican History of Art", Published in 1953 by Penguin Books, 512 pages.*

3. *Ananda K Coomarswamy, "History of Indian and Indonesian Art", Published in 1966, by Dover Publications Inc. New York. 295pages+XVIIIpages*

4. *Mathuram Bhoothalingam, "Temples of India, Myths and Legends", Published in 1986, by Publication Division, Ministry of Information and Broadcasting, Govt. of India.*

5. *C Sivaramamurti. "Indian Painting", Published in 1970 by National Book Trust, India, 132 pages.*

6. *Vasudeva Agrawala, "The Heritage of Indian Art, A Pictorial Presentation". Published in 1986 by Publication Division, Govt. of India. 186 pages.*

7. *Articles by various writers on "Modernism and Bombay Progressive Art Group and Group 1890" in Lalitkala Contemporary 2, 22 and 31 in 1963, 1978 and 1990 respectively by Central Lalitkala Academi, New Delhi.*

8. *Various Writers, "Bendre: The Painter and the Person", Published in 1990 by Bendre Foundation for art and culture and the Indus Corporation, 210 pages.*

9. *Mildred Archer, "India and British Portraiture, 1770-1825", Published in 1979 by Oxford University Press.296pages.*

10. *R P Gupta, "Some British and European Painters in India, 1760-1850". Published in 1979 by Times of India in its Annual.*

11. *Philip S Rawson, edited by Pierre Tisme, "Indian Painting" Published in 1970 by Universe Books Inc. New York.*

12. *Chintamonikar, Yogesh Chandra Bagal and Mukul Dey "School of Industrial Art 1865, College of Art and Craft 1951 at Calcutta", published in 1966 by College of Art Calcutta. 217pages.*

13. *Prodosh Das Gupta, "Calcutta Group Manifesto", Published in 1970 by Artist's Group at Calcutta.*

14. *Articles in publication "Trends Art Magazine' published from Cholalmandalam Artists Village, Chennai.*

15. *"Nandan" Annuals published in Santiniketan during Nandan Mela each year*

Societal Situations underneath Craft Ethnicity in Kerala

Abstract: the geographical situation of Kerala has an important role in contributing to a variety of craft forms. Four-caste system is the social strategy that supported the creation of craft forms in Kerala. There are several particular caste formations specified in production of typical style of craft productions. Practice of Makhathayam and Marumakhathayam developed special strategies within the society. The craft production was highly influenced by practice of Makhatthayam and Marumakhathayam - two kinds of ancestral economic management systems.

Key words: Humanitarian, Creativity, Society, Four caste System, Makhattayam, Marumakhattayam, Craft Forms.

Introduction: Kerala is situated in the far south of India facing the Arabian Sea and shares the border with Karnataka and Tamil Nadu. There are several craft forms prevalent in Kerala which receives pampering from unique social situations persisting there. These craft activities are shaped with the acceptance of current social circumstances prevailing there as a continuation of societal activity formations from the past. These productions are results of persisting demands from the society for such objectivities. Scenario of social life forms the platform for active participation of these objectivities in humanitarian spaces. Such demands are forwarded through special roles of typical objectivities in social life practice and through social life. This special active role is generated through habits of the society with its own social limitations, like behavioral attitudes, habitual practices, availability of natural resources, and explorations like economical situations, philosophical awareness, devotional practice, psychological ambience or religious participatory activities. Each of the times these craft forms took form of life even without acknowledgement of social plants with which they are attached but justified its social relevance and absolute necessity of getting it shaped as it is.

It is very interesting to note that beliefs have an important role in the 'social beingness' of mankind. First of all, formation of caste system is an important phenomenon that took spontaneous generation in the humanitarian social tedium. Man explored his potentials as a living creature with understandings about the process of existence (practice of life). Man recognized limitations of his materialistic remaining and ideological set up of the mind. The abilities are recognized by its individual (personality of ability) during vesting of an action in the society in a specific form on social requirement of its procession and it's potentials of creativity, physical strength and natural abilities were remarkably identified and evaluated in society. These typical elements prepared actor's psychological platform to discriminate human groups which has different habits from the others.

Various sub caste formations and its relevance: Establishment of four caste system and its active role in society are on special concern here in these notes. The caste system protracted in Kerala is an extension of four caste system that prevailed in India for several past centuries. The social situation in Kerala was an extension of the similar conditions prevailed in the rest of this geographical area. There were four castes were formed according to each ones special role in the society, 1. Brahmins- the priestly caste that handled all devotional requirements of the society. 2. Kshathriyas-the ruling people who acquired all powers and controls over the existing behaviors of the society. 3. Vaysyas-the economic manipulators of the society who controlled all business objectivities. and 4. Shudras the group of people dedicated to the cultivation and related activities for rest of the people in the society.[1]

In practice of four caste system there are several definite differences originated within the social mortality of the above noted four major categories. The Shudras are most relevant here because they are the working class which included largest number of people in the society. This social group included producers of food grains, involved in fabrication of residences, house making and keeping, worked to breed animals, drove the vehicles, worked to satisfy all and intact painstaking facility and its requirements of the society. Being deserted by the rest of the higher caste patterns of the society due to the superiority avowed by them, the works inferiors engaged were never considered major. Within the lucidly fabricated social strata, other three categories Brahmins, Kshathriyas, and Vyshyas were industrious against extravagant major works implicated by the society. Gathering social acceptance for such discriminative systematic development continued in the society for several centuries and began to be considered as a genuine humanitarian feature.

There are several categories identified within caste positions of Shudras the very last location in four caste system. The human wherewithal who did précised works on wood for the construction of houses, furniture, wood works for shelters like residences to big palaces, devotional venues like temples, and gathering atmospheres for social purposes- were categorized as "asari"[2] means the carpenter. The people who undertook other masonry works of above noted suburban areas were known as "mesthry"[2] means the Mason. The people who belonged to the job in which "Moosha"[2] has important role was titled as "moosharis"[2]. Moosha is the fireplace for the heavy work including works for utensils on metals like brass, copper and bonze. The workers prepared Moosha the mere exact emptiness of the objectivity proposed to be made with solid sustenance and mixture of different metals, poured in to them (consolidated emptiness) for creation of constructive enormity including Utensils and other objects. mooshari polished them to increase its softness and beauty before marketing, production and marketing of which made their livelihood.

The jewelry maker uses small iron hammers and node with them to the seasoned gold for shaping it to beautiful jewelries. He uses small furnace by keeping half burned coconut shelves on a terracotta vase, in order to make his purpose fit. Nodding is called in Malayalam language "Thattuka"[3]. The person practices "That" (Node) are called "Thattan" (Nodder)[3]. Thattan is a caste in Kerala engaged in making of jewellery. It required further studies to state from which form of four caste system the Thattan is generated because the current "Thattan" is found even from Brahmin caste with Tamil relations. This might have happened because the fascination on gold by human generations through all past centuries around the globe. Gold is considered for purity and heavenliness. All job related with god is supposed to be done by Brahmins by the ancient protocols of the four caste system. However the members from families of Thattan sub caste have traditionally acquired the ability for making Jewelry from ancestors and it is considered as a traditional job.

Similarly the works related with devotional purposes are generally deposited to the higher categorical phenomenon. Continuation to establishment of caste system in Indian scenario, in Kerala the highest cast known is Brahmins and the next Caste acquired higher social status is Kshathriyas. Locally, Brahmins are called Namboothiri and Khathriyas as Varmas. Khathriyas took configuration in Kerala with family relationship of Brahmins. As a matter of fact Brahmins had relationship with other castes in the society. The hereditary production of Brahmins with caste people of lower status in the society made an in between caste "Nair"[4] in Kerala. Their social status was never up to Brahmin or Kshathriyas. Nair families had relations with both Royal families and Brahmin families but social setup never permitted to conduct job of the both strata. As a matter of fact Nair families acquired land ownership of large areas by having relations with both ruling caste families and priestly families. To them always economy and land ownership of the society were attributed. They majorly turned cultivation motivators with necessary power for it as they acquired ownership of large cultivation areas.

All of these were results of changes in the society due to practice of "Makkathayam and Marumakkathayam." In Makkathayam[5] when the rights go to the biological children, the rights are handed over to in-laws after the death of power gatherer in Marumakkathayam. When the Marumakkathayam[5] was on practice the rights went to the women and her children who got married to the eldest son of the family. When Makkathayam was the system followed by Brahmin families, Marumakkathayam was practiced by Nair families. The sons except the eldest one was not permitted to marry from same caste in Brahmin families during ancient period. So the other sons found his spouse from Nair families or even from lower caste families where as the girl children of the family had all rights through Makkathayam. The Brahmin who gets married from Nair families held all functions of his life in his spouse house after marriage and returned his body for burial to his home after his death, where his spouse is not permitted to enter due to un- touch-ability which on practice. His children are never considered in the home of his father but live their lives in mother's house. This was the situation in Nair families even hardly a century ago. Due to the reason of having relation with Brahmin families, the Nair families acquired special status in the society, since the Brahmin were highly considered as they were at higher most consideration in caste ideals because of priestly engagements. They were considered purer than any of other castes and engaged them comes in the outside labors of the temples including cleaning temple premises, preparing for worship, making garlands for idols etc without any gender differences.

There were some new caste formations according to the work they engaged in temples. The people of the family who were engaged in making garlands and other similar jobs were known as Warriers[6] and the people who made pictures on the floor with color powders were established as Kurup[7] families. The meaning of 'Kurickuka' in Malayalam is "making marks". The men who make marks on the floor in temple began to be established as Kurup- the man who makes marks. Even currently making of diagrams on floor and worship to the relevant god or goddess is considered as a devotional right of such families.

A well known festival is held at Vaikkom Mahadeva[8] Temple where the deity is Lord Siva. Lord Shiva generated Bhadrakali to end the mischievous, troublesome, and cruel activities of Darika the Asura the anti human activist, to satisfy Goddess Bhadrakali for the goodness of human. It began to worship Bhadrakali every twelve years, by drawing her gigantic images in the North East corner of outside premises at the very famous Vaikkom Mahadeva Temple. The devotees draw the iconographic image of Bhadrakali with vegetable colors and worship through song accompanied by village instruments. During the Bhadrakalikalam deliberation, the eldest person of Puthussery Kurup family starts the drawing, known as Kalam kurikkal. (Kalam Kurup).[9] It is the right of the Puthussery Kurup family to begin the drawing on floor, fill it with colors, and sing the devotional song with accompaniment of musical instruments. The eldest person from the Kurup family will lead the entire program and complete at the end by removing it.

In some temples the Marar[10] family members are also engaged in similar works related with devotional matters such as garland making with flowers, Horning (Blowing) the conch in necessary intervals of worship and playing (blow) percussion instrument like Chenda in times, ringing the temple bells and help the main priest by drawing various designs for Pujas, Cleaning the temple premises etc. But in the case of snake Goddess worships; the people who belong to the sub caste 'Pulluvar'[11] were responsible for drawing the picture and worship by singing songs of praises. 'Pulluvar' belonged to "Shudras" in four caste system.

In certain areas of Kerala (Palghat) performing with leather puppetteering prevails as a practice of devotional offering the Lordess Bhadrakali. Puppets are made by drawing the images on deer leather, color and cut them according to generate necessary images for manipulation, make mobility on them by necessary techniques and project them in mobilization to a cotton cloth curtain with help of shadows generated by use of oil lamps. It is accompanied by verbal music with musical instruments. The artists are belongs to nomadic families who migrated from place to place during past several centuries. They speak their own language "araa'[12] at home but the language of verbal music describing story killing Darikasura (demon Darika) is in Tamil. They are vegetarian families, purely devotional, depend up on public performances and assigned performances with receiving payments. These people belongs to the caste similar to 'Vellalar'[13] sub caste in Kerala but Vellalar did not consider them equal because of Tamil relations of puppet maker families. Any how it can be assumed that they are basically from 'Shudra' caste of the four caste system.

The terracotta workers traditionally belong to a caste known as 'Kusava'[14] and are vegetarians for several generations. The particular caste people are responsible for making terracotta utensils and other images for the entire society. They are vegetarians like the Brahmin caste people but they are not accepted with social status of Brahmins except they could wear a sacred thread on their shoulder. As a matter of fact they get acceptance equal to Shudras, since they are very much associated with working class of people. Their work is generally included with immense of human labor in it. It requires utilizing human power to collect clay from the surroundings by digging wet grounds and paste it with smashing by foot. They make the collected clay sufficiently pasty enough to mould utensils, create utensils with use of a turning mechanical potter's wheel, put the images in shadows to dry, beat them in to accurate shape and fire the kiln using wooden logs to bake. In each step of the entire work of terracotta utensils making requires human labor - the hard continuous work is unavoidable.

There are other social requirements in Kerala like making cloth, is also highly involved by workers who belong to Shudra caste orientation like all other above noted specified works from centuries ago. Neythu[15] is the Malayalam word for weaving and the people engaged in such work are noted by Neythukar, the weavers. They are spread all over Kerala and it a mixed commune- people belonging to various levels of caste system is regularly engaged in such works. Weaving is time consuming and laborious work in which all members of the family partake with their special interests in various levels of weaving work with the use of a locally handmade mechanism called Thary.

Another fully developed orientation we see all over Kerala is the continuation of Mural tradition in Kerala. The paintings are done on temple walls of Kerala, with accuracy in connecting the images with Puranic recourses.[16] Natural colors are used for the painting process on the walls of Garbha Griha (Sanctum Sanctorium) where the images of God or Goddesses are kept. As a matter of fact the interiors of Hindu temples were never opened for mixed commune of Kerala before Temple Proclamation[17]. It is clear that the paintings on the walls of temple were painted by artists belongs to higher castes like Kurup, Marar, Nair etc. Currently we could see that people belonging to mixed communal entities are involved in the act of painting as it is a highly appreciated profession and a professional teaching subject in Universities. Also this is important to note that currently all kinds of jobs are engaged by people who belongs to all different communities and different life styles, who are accepted in the new social circumstances. One can easily find a person who belongs to Muslim caste orientation busy with carpentry works for fabrication of huge ships on wood in northern Kerala and the people belongs to Christian beliefs are famed as Bronze Bell makers with wide social acceptance. The craft production is out of all centuries old caste demarcations and it is only the quality of production is under consideration.

Conclusion: There are several sub caste formations based on the work they are engaged in, currently existing in the Kerala society but they are exempted describing here due to irrelevance in current topic of discussion. The incident of 1947[18] changed the shape of all caste differentiations and it overtook the changes contributed by all various social reform movements. Indian Constitution took its shape with birth of independence from the rule of British. Article fifteen of that Indian Constitution abandoned celebration of discrimination on the grounds of caste and race.

As per the calculations, in 2003, Govt. of Kerala recognized fifty three Scheduled Castes, thirty five Scheduled Tribes and eighty other Backwards Classes.[19] About ten percentage of population belongs to sixty eight various Scheduled Castes as in 2001 during Census of India. Among the total communities there were ninety nine point nine percentages was Hindu, with a countable number of Sikhs and Buddhists in it.[20] Thirty five Scheduled tribes are recognized by Census conducted and a little more than one percentage of Scheduled Tribe people among a total of which ninety four percentages of people belongs to Hindu religion. The rest included less than six percentages of Christians and remaining the Muslims.[20]

In new social atmosphere and social conditions the caste oriented professional practice turned meaningless and citizens of India began to enjoy regulations singly maintained in our nation. All job practices began to get acceptance only on the basis of merits on particular work. Apart from engaging on work of interest the workers acquired working knowledge from traditional family background continued the exploration to their wisdom.

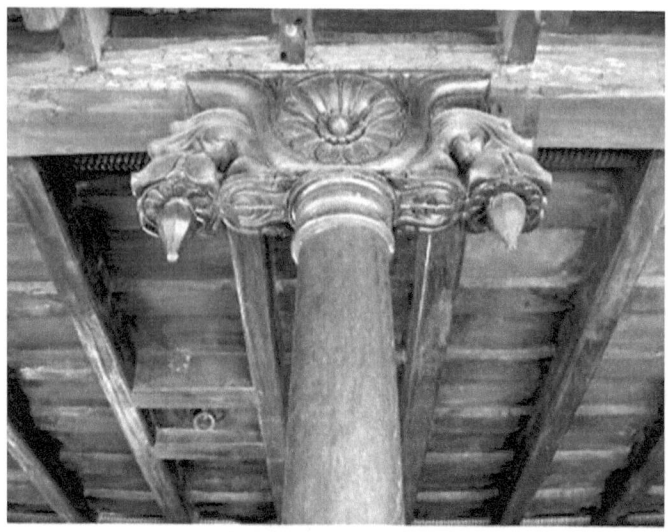

Evidence of elaborate wood work, Ceiling at Padamanabhapuram Palace supported with decorative pillar.

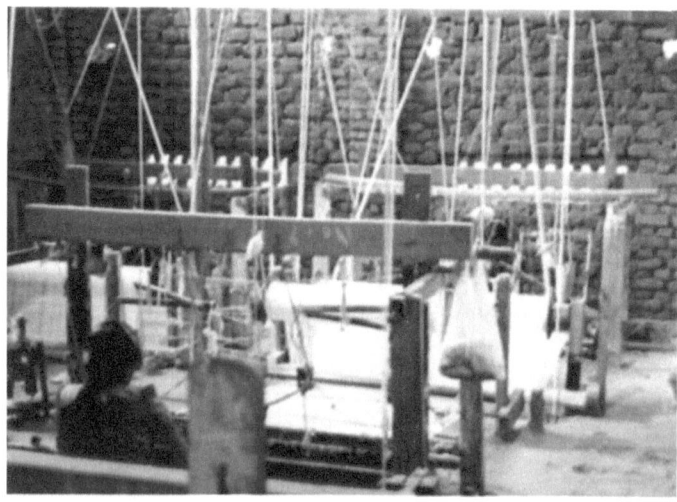

Weaving on progress in a pitloom.

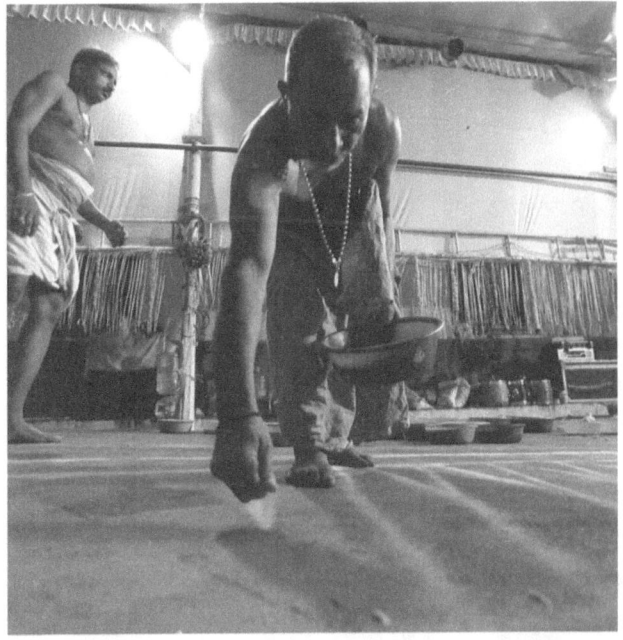

Gopalakrishna Kurup of Puthussery Family performing Kalam
Kurikkal.

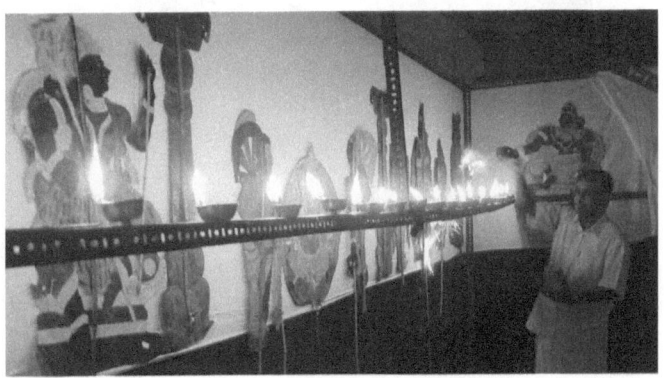

Artist at performance with leather puppets in Kerala

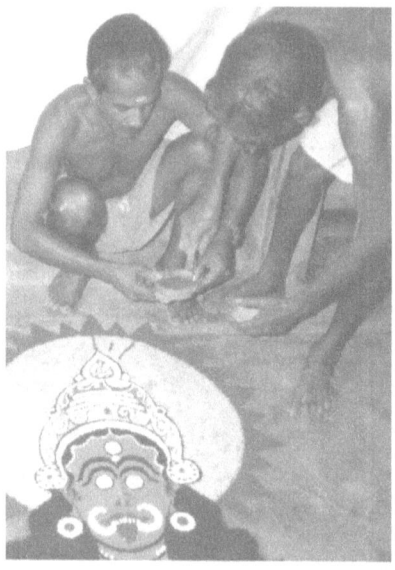

Achutha Paniker and his disciple working for a Bhadrakalikalam in a devotional space.

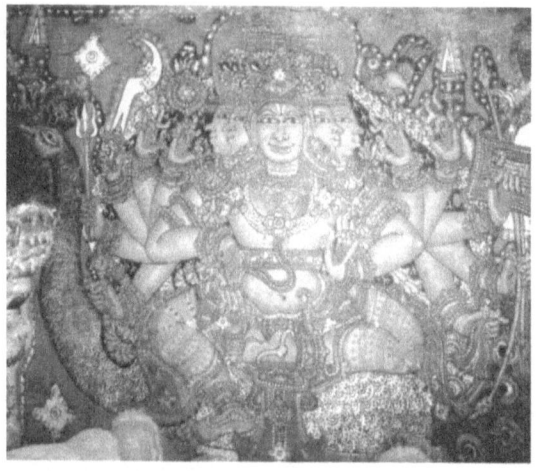

Image of Shanmukha at Haripad Keezhtrikkovil drawn according to Puranic references.

Photography: *Courtesy- Images 2,3,4,. Babu Namboodiri K Photography 2003, Image-8. Suresh, Punalur photography 1990, Image 10. Supported by, Ramachandra Pulavar.*

Notes

1. *Typical implementation of Four Caste System. Society is divided in to four according to the social requirement of workers in various fields of human life.*
2. *Asari, Mestry, Moosha and Mooshari are Malayalam words by origin. It means Carpenter, Mason, Mold and Molding persons respectively.*
3. *Thattuka and Thattan are Malayalam words means Nodd and Nodder respectively. and Gold smith is the equal word in English.*
4. *Nair is an in between caste. Their position is between Brahmin and Kshathriya communes. Kept strong and family relations with both communes and acquired high social status in the society.*
5. *In makkhatthayam, the sons and daughters get the power in various angleson demise of the wealthy parents. But in Marumakhatthayam the rights goes to in-laws who marry the son or daughter.*
6. *Warrier is again an ambalavasi family.*
7. *Kurikkuka is draw the image is in Malayalam. As person who draws the image in powder colors may be called Kurup to connect him with the event.*
8. *Vaikkam Mahaveva Temple is well known venue of devotional practices for past several centuries*
9. *Read Note number 7and 8.*
10. *Marar is another famous Temple Caste, who majorly involve in temple works like garland making and cleaning*

jobs of the temple premises. They are with equal status of Nair in society but more divinity is claimed due to engagements in temple related heavenly jobs.

11. *Pulluvar is belonged Shudra commune of Four Caste system, their devotional practices were different until they began to be permitted to enter in Temples by Temple Proclamation of Balarama Varna Maharaja of Travancore, which permitted all Hindu caste believers to enter temples. Pulluvar sing songs to satisfy Snake Goddesses with accompaniment of certain musical instruments. After Temple Proclamation we saw them conducting worship of their Gods and Goddesses within temple premises.*

12. *Aara, is a mixed Language used by leather puppeteers in their home to communicate with their family members.*

13. *Vellalar of Kerala does not agree with it equal status of puppeteers due puppeteers Tamil relations.*

14. *Kusavas of Kerala are sharing equal social status of Shudras, claims equal status with Brahmins because they are vegetarians and wear sacred thread for centuries.*

15. *Neythu, and Neythukar in Malayalam means Weaving and weavers respectively.*

16. *Creating Mural painting on walls Kerala Temples with vegetable colors is a tradition of several centuries.. More than 170 venues were marked with presence of stylistic mural painting in Kerala.*

17. *Temple proclamation declared right of all Hindus without any discrimination to enter temples for devotional purposes. His highness Sree Chithira Thirunal Balarama Varma Maha Raja of Travancore Kingdom on his 24 the birthday in 1936 made the announcement of Temple*

Proclamation bill which gathered wide appreciation for its humanitarian approach.

18. *Independence marks the end of British rule in 1947 and the establishment of a free and independent Indian nation which marked a sea of changes in lives.*

19. *As referred in Wikipedia "Official. Archived from the original on 15 February 2008.*

20. *As referred in Wikipedia "Data Highlights: The Scheduled Castes". Census of India 2001. 27 March 2007. Retrieved 8 November 2011.*

References

Selected Readings only

1. *"Kerala." Encyclopeedia Britannica. Encyclopeadia Britannica Online. Encyclopeedia Britannica Inc., 2011. Web. 26 December 2011.*

2. *S. Ramachandran Nair, Freedom Struggle in Colonial Kerala, Published in Kalady. Pages 186.*

3. *Sreedhara Menon, A. (2008). Kerala History and its Makers. DC Books*

4. K N Panikkar, Essays on the History and Society of Kerala, K N Panikkar, Kerala Council for Historical Research.

5. *Pupul Jayakar "The Earthern Drum". IGNCA. 1982. Pages 480.*

6. *Sreedhara Menon (2008). Cultural Heritage of Kerala. D C Books.*

7. *Elements of Hindu Iconography by Mr. Gopinath Rao, Page 142*

8. *Folk art of Bengal" by Ajith Mukherjee. Page 221*

9. *Dr. M G Sasi Bhooshan. Keraliya Kala Darsanam, Kerala State Institute of Languages. 2001.*

10. *Dr. M G Sasi Bhooshan. Karalathile Chuvar Chithrangal, Kerala State Institute of Langages. Pages-240.*

11. *Babu Namboodiri K, Our Traditional Leather Shadow Puppeteers. Melinda Books, 2018. Pages. 156.*

A Variety of Ethnicities on Craft Conception Habituated in Premises of Kerala

Abstract: *There are a number of conformist skill based forms extensively prevalent in instantaneous circumstances clearly visible for ordinary human beings. As a matter of fact, these innovative forms are part of an average power of human survival and performances of these social mechanisms are unavoidable for its existence. Many mechanisms are invented for reducing difficulties of employment and with the use of them strains are evacuated to negligible. Apart from useful aspects common man like them to contain a shape that enhances the aesthetic sensibilities of its beholder. On anticipation of this specific utility these mechanisms are well planned before creation. There are several activities that come into ones purview when it's seriously looked upon for its significance. In this study several venues of craft production are elaborately explained and its social relevance on materialistic and aesthetic utility is pointed out. The craft productions found in Kerala has two phases, the first* *one is with excess of labor content in it and other is with more aesthetic or philosophic content. Necessity of further studies in this area is exposed and confirmed.*

Key words: Asari, Kollan, Nalukettu, Chathurvarnya, Mushari, Kumbhakar, Thadukku, Aattavilakku, Shadow Puppets, Bhadrakalikalam, Mural painting, Weavers.

Introduction: There are several conventional craft forms widespread in our instant situations which are observable for ordinary human being. As a matter of reality, these creative forms are part of an average fortitude and performances of these social mechanisms are unavoidable for any survival. Man invented mechanisms for reducing his hazardousness of employment and composed their physical strains negligible. Apart from serviceable aspects the man likes them to contain a shape appealing to his aesthetic sensibilities. So he began to create with planned observations, anticipations and predictions. Anticipation is a humanitarian behavior, he self accessed its explicitly beneficial efficiency and he cheerfully acknowledged the unintentional temperament of it. There are several of activities that come into ones purview when seriously look up for its significance.

Certain Objects and objectivities: Implementation of wheel by its nature of revolving dynamics is one of the above noted kinds of finding. Colloquially called "Kappi" (means pully) for the wheel made out of wooden logs placed over deep wells in villages all over Kerala is an example. It resides as a most major mechanism found by human being, remained usable for several centuries and famed for its straight forwardness and novel nature. These wheels are made in both materials, wood and iron. The wheels that are made in wood are always made by craft persons belonged to carpenter families generally called "Asari"[1] which is a job associated caste name in Kerala. If this mechanism is fully made with solid iron, then the creator would be an Iron worker who is called "Kollan"[2] (Blacksmith) in Kerala villages.

Another most significant example for a craft tradition that has been carried out for several centuries and made its impact stationary in our social background is the use of Bullock Carts. The huge, more than 6 feet dimensioned circular wheels are made up of wood and placed in both sides of the wooden platform created to place heavy materials measuring tons. An elongated wooden part is placed from the centre portion of the bullock cart in front. This portion is attached with two powerful bulls permitting them to pull the cart filled with heavy materials or the number of people who sat on them including the driver who controls the bulls. Majorly wood is the material used for the preparation of bullock carts and carpenters belonged to "Asari" caste families are the creators of the same.

The workers related with "Asari" caste families have remarkable contributions on preparation of furniture for various purposes including chairs, cots, tables, other such objects and wardrobes. Apart from major masonry craft persons, it requires specially trained workers belonging to 'Asari' caste for preparation of a house for construction of which wood is utilized as the major material. Whatever may be the material for construction, it was the duty of carpenter to make necessary calculations, create the concept and design for the building in Kerala, and he took the entire role of an architect during construction. With knowledge acquired traditionally on architecture they built beautiful houses using natural wood and named them Nalukettu, Ettukettu or Pathinarukettu according to the size of the houses they made. When the walls of the houses were made on wooden pedestals the rooms were called "Ara"[3]. Nalukettu (Four Blocks) is a house built with buildings in four sides, Ettukettu (Eight Blocks) is with adjunct of such two structures for single house and PatinaruKettu (sixteen blocks) is construction of sixteen blocks which enables four top open central portions in the single residential building. The number of people could be accommodated in each style of building is increased as per the number of kettu (Block) is increased. Beautiful carvings on wood are elaborately chiseled to decorate various portions of the Padmanabhapuram[4] Palace is an example, for such kinds of residential buildings built in various parts of Kerala.

Single blocks are made for single family houses and four block houses with single opening at the central portion (Nalukettu) are built for the use of big joint family houses. Ettukettu of eight structures are built for rich family houses for accommodating large number of people in it and Pathinarukettu are built for even bigger number of people, accommodated rich joint families and also the palaces. Palace of Attingal[5] is such a building traditionally made centuries ago but currently some parts of this structure is partially rebuilt or demolished forever.

There are beautiful carvings made on wood that are deliberately used in various parts of the buildings in Kerala. These kinds of deliberations are visible all over the building particularly in which the wood is the major material. Decoratively carved portions are situated even in the roof structures made up of wood, specially designed carvings along the sides of wooden doors, pillars and supporting beams etc. The pillars are decorated with Corinthian Capitals most of the time if it is in the open areas in the centre portions of the Nalukettu.

The central joining portions of the two shutters of doors are covered by a thick wooden log which is generally decorative all the time. It has no other function than to become supportive to the shutters. The central portions of the door are fitted with huge iron lock which is usually has curiously curved portions which generate curiosity of the viewers. The people belonging to "Kollan" religious group were responsible for making of all iron tools starting from small knives known as penknives to axe called Kodali[6], the heaviest tool to cut wood. They were skilled enough people to meet all iron work demands including sharpening tools, making small mechanisms in locks, designing beautiful locks and Making tools for carpenters, stone workers and all other tools, arms and armories to maintain ordinary life in a village. It is here important to state that the sub castes Asari Musari Karuvan and Thattan are subdivisions of Viswakarma the splendid division of Sudra and the fourth division of Chathurvarnya[7] society.

People of "Mushari" religious division were responsible for all works related with casting and making of utensils. Copper, brass and bronze were three different mixtures of metals used for such purposes in Kerala. Uruli, Valkindi, Thalika, Poothalam, Traditional Lamps known as Nilavilakku[8] are some of such utility objects made with devotional purposes and revered utilities. The workers of the village in this particular category have always adopted the lost wax method for the creation of casted utensils in Kerala. Kodivilakku[8] is a small lamp used during devotional practices, use of which is largely appreciated in temple surroundings. The devotional bell is another object used during devotional practices. The traditional bronze bells are made in various sizes and with various combinations of metals for the creation of desired tune from it. Similarly the lamps, utensils such as Lotta, Uruli, Kindi are made in various sizes to support the day to day utility. Traditional Lamps are made in various sizes up to more than six feet heights which are utilized during Kathakali performances in Kerala and were known as Aattavilakku[9].

The workers belonging o Kubhakar[10] sub-cast were responsible for making terracotta utensils in villages. They collect clay from loose soiled cultivation fields and smash over it after mixing with fibrous materials to generate pasty quality and boldness. They make the utensils using this pasty clay and broaden them by putting in sunlight. They beat over the form and tight the clay broadens and let it fully dry in shadows. Later they are burnt on fire and the shapes are made permanent. It was on practice and the products were on sale by the producers themselves travelling by foot taking them in heavy baskets over head.

There are several kinds of baskets for carrying objects that are made using prepared bamboo flexible strips. The largest of them which are meant to carry heavy articles, are made considerably big and are called 'Kutta'[11]. They are popularly used in entire Kerala. The ordinary people place heavy objects in "Kutta" and carry those over head for transportation. Thick bamboo splits are the material used by the workers who make it. Similarly small baskets are made to carry small objects and keep them in homes, which are called "Vatti"[11]. Most of the time bamboo split is the material for production of the "Vattis". Bamboo split is made thin and cleaned to make flattened square holders by hand weave to create "Muram"[11]. It is largely used in all over Kerala state to handle rice and paddy. "Parambu"[11] is a larger mat weaved using bamboo thin material which is largely on use in Kerala to place paddy and rice on sun light. The Parambu are rolled longer and hung in village houses for future uses over several years.

But it can be noticed that there are 'Vattis' made with prepared soft materials made from other vegetations too. Same material is used for the preparation of mats to lie on which are sized normally 6 feet x 3 feet. Sometimes prepared leaf of "palm tree" (Panamaram) is used to prepare small bags. Same material is used to make small mats for sitting on the floor which are known as "Thadukku"[11].

There are Umbrellas made using prepared leaves of "Palm Tree" which are made round and conical in shape, could be fitted on head so the user didn't have to carry it. There are even smaller umbrellas made with a bamboo handle. The raw rice measuring vessels and small measuring vessels are made both in metal and wood. They are widely available all through Kerala. Wooden seats to sit are of a special mobile design widely used in Kerala. Another remarkable utility based production is Maruvis[11] made out of wood. Also the Aattukallu, Arakalllu,[11] grounding mechanism trough turning etc made up of granite are wonderful human inventions were the brain took its role soundly.

The mechanisms used for removing water shed from the cultivation fields in farm bound wet areas of Kerala are also to be considered here. I have already discussed a number of venues where craft production conceived on the basis of utility. Apart from materialistic utility the man has demands for objects useful to his psychological leisure. Belief in religion is reason to substitute leisure, an unavoidable element in human lives. To accommodate leisure, human mind search for departed feeling from his busy schedules of workouts in day to day life. They curiously found religious reasons to produce objectivities which have no other meanings than production of aesthetics and leisure. The society found logical conclusions for involvement in mind simulative activities like creation of aesthetic objectivities in collection of massive efforts.

All along Kerala, beautiful pedestals are made during festivals of temples and otherwise, and are carried on with massive efforts by large number of people gathered on religious reasons, considering the temple of deity the destination. Thousands of people are gathered for such functions on particular days and time as they make it as a purpose of duty. These images have more to do than just appealing aesthetic sensibilities, but the rest is psychological and indescribable. The pedestals made during the Bharani festival of Chettikulangara[12] temple are an objectivity of this kind. Several Pedestals are made by different groups of people and brought them to the temple premises with participation of human gathering. Such kinds of forms are made all over Kerala in relation with temple festivals and the entire process is done with large human attention and participation in each venue. Similarly, animal figures are made in huge sizes, decorated and carried to festival venues with logics build on religious themes. These animal figures are known as "Kuthira"[13] in the villages. Chinakkathur Pooram and Machathu Mamangam are some notable occasions of this kind. The various images of "Theyyam" are a good example of elaborate craft attempts made by human being for other than mere utility purposes but devotional and aesthetics.

Shadow puppeteering[14] is an entirely unique production with ambience of aesthetics and leisure. There are more than 150 venues in Kerala where shadow puppeteering is held during festivals as a yearly practice particularly in northern parts of Kerala. Puppets are made with prepared animal leather and colored with natural colors. The shadows are projected to a cotton screen with moving effect and religious story is narrated dramatically and musically with accompaniment of musical instruments. Basically the men behind it are nomads, roots found all over the globe. There are a number of families settled currently in Kerala for past several centuries' finds reasonable reasons for their century long stay here. In India, they generally adapt the story of Ramayana as a major theme for theatrical presentation which is largely appreciated.

Widely spread all over Kerala is the drawing with vegetable powder colors and worship of particular god or goddess for blessings on anticipation of advancement in life. Most popular one among such craft production is Bhadrakali kalamezhuthu[15] and singing of praises of Goddess. The biggest diagrams in this style are done once in 12 years at Vaikkam Mahadeva Temple along with other worship modes, which are known as Vadakkupurathu Pattu. This is a 12 days long celebration during which variant iconographic images of Goddess are drawn each day which shows the arrival of Lordess Bhadrakali on Vetal - her chariot- with the head of Darikasura (Darika the demon) on her hand after killing him on a fierce war. Praising songs to Bhadrakali is sung in the evenings after drawing the images and the picture is removed at the end by the devotees. Removed mixed color powder is distributed as Prasad to devotees. There are many hundreds of venues in Kerala where similar kinds of devotional practices are performed to attract well wishers of Devi for goodness of Man.

There are more than two hundred venues marked in Kerala where Mural paintings are elaborately drawn. The surfaces of the devotional venues are prepared for painting and pictures are drawn with naturally produced colors. Most of the time Hindu religious themes are stylistically drawn on the walls of temples.[16] Pictures were drawn several centuries ago. When Christianity was established in Kerala, the churches also began to be decorated with these kinds of narrative pictures. It is important to note that the oldest examples for these painting activities might have been done by higher caste Hindu artists belonging to sub castes of Nair like Warrier, Kurup, Marar[17] etc, because entrance of lower and other caste people were largely controlled before Temple Proclamation in 1936. Most of the meticulously done venues were created before that.

The people who survived at the northern coastal areas of Kerala are experts in making huge ships which are practically found beneficial and economically supportive. Local technologies are utilized and they build big ships using wood as a major material and market them as requirement. There are several families and groups in Kerala dedicatedly working in this area of craft production.

There are several thousands of humans engaged in making cloth by hand weaving. Balaramapuram[18] of southern Kerala is an example for such venues in Kerala. Hand weavers are spread all over Kerala and mostly they are belongs to lower caste Hindu Families. It required more than one person efforts to continue cloth production by hand weaving and it a joined process. Many of the time all the family members are involved with various stages of cloth production including arranging the fibre, weaving, Coloring and marketing. They are bound to enquire other resources also for a stable survival as the wages in this area of production are very low. Also currently the hand weavers have to compete with cloth mills, their massive low cost production and marketing skills.

Conclusion: In this study, I have briefly introduced and explained several venues of craft production which has social relevance on materialistic and aesthetic utility. The craft productions found in Kerala has two phases, the first one is with excess of labor content in it and other is with more aesthetic or philosophic content. The later discussed craft forms like leather puppet manipulating, mural painting, and the festival images (forms made and carried by human gatherings during festivals) have a greater affinity towards production of visual aesthetics. But as a matter of fact productions in these titles are just making repetitions of the images previously done with neglecting the spirit of making aesthetic saturated and secondary by some of them acquire and reflects the meaning that certain level of practice could make anybody a creator of this genre. But it is true only when considering materialistic but untrue for creation of artists of improvisation and experimentation. They could only produce craft but not aesthetics. After several centuries of continuous work they are unable to mark any kind of improvised status in their products. The forces of widely accepted art forms are their capacity for renovation and originality on mere communication. But many times images are not created for communication of aesthetics and realities of life but to transfer religious content and physical being in it as a mere and only purpose, as it is a craft form which has to meet its mere purposes only. The innocent repetitive qualities with focus on results are never vanishing but powerfully reminding its weaknesses to turn original. Thus it found adequate to attach them into category of crafts than original unique art form.

I have described all what is naturally exposed to as craft production after evaluation by analyzing them in various grounds by being a curious resident of this area. So the necessity of further studies in this area is exposed and confirmed.

Image: Courtesy: *images1-10, 14,15, 22-26 common files widely available used, Images 11,12,13,27, and 28 Artist Babunamboodiri K photography 2014 and 2003, Images 16-18 Support from Ramachandra Pulavar, 20 Suresh Punalur Photography, Images 19, 21 image supported by Vaikkom Gopalakrishna Kurup.*

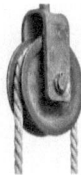 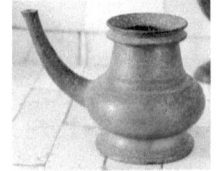 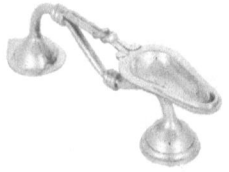

Iron Kappi (Pully). Kindi, Kodivilakku.

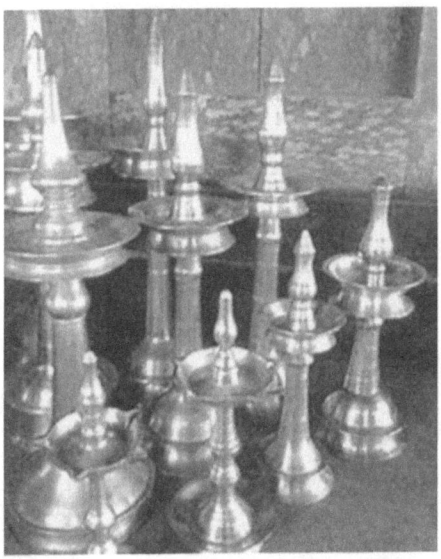

Traditional lamp- Nila Vilakku - Various sizes.

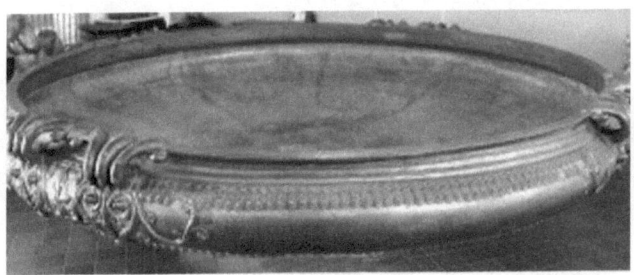

Warpu, a bronze casted utensil for cooking food for feasts.

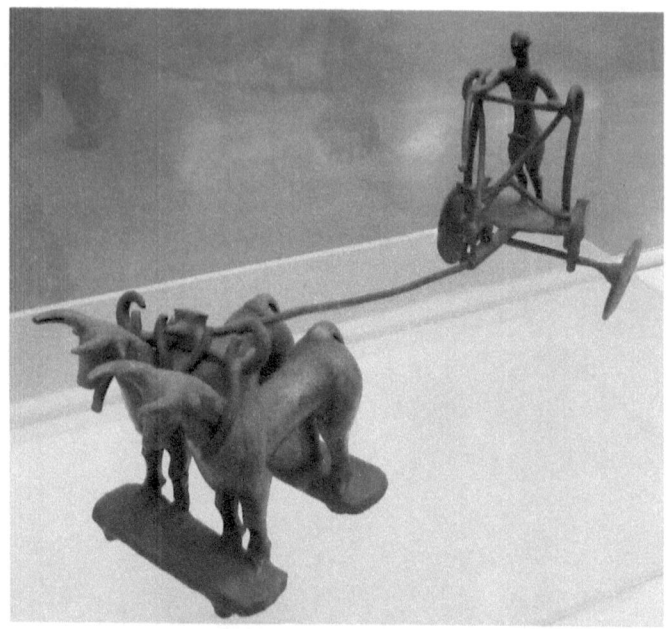

Bullock Cart, a terracotta representation from Indus valley.

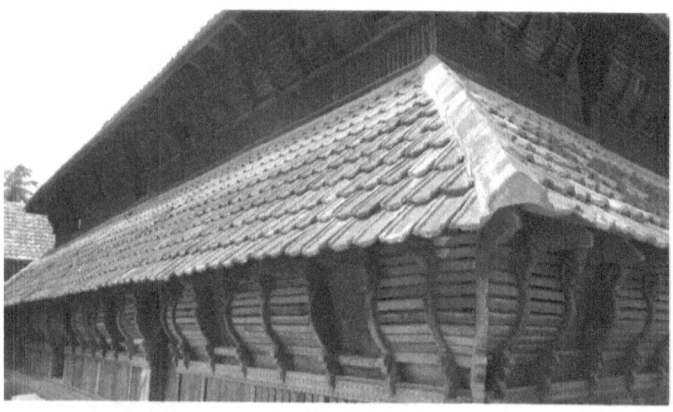

Portion of Padmanabhapuram palace example for Kerala Architecture.

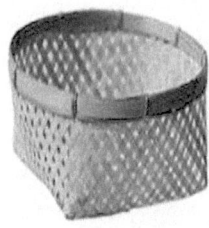 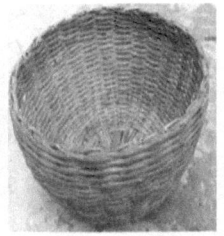 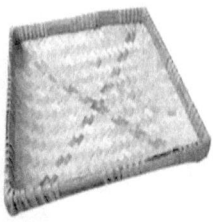

Vatti, Kutta, Muram for handling household items.

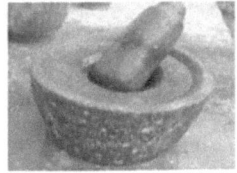 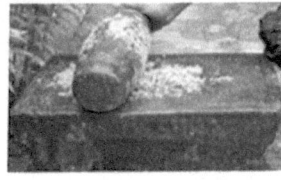 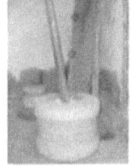

Aattukallu, Arakallu, Ural for household use.

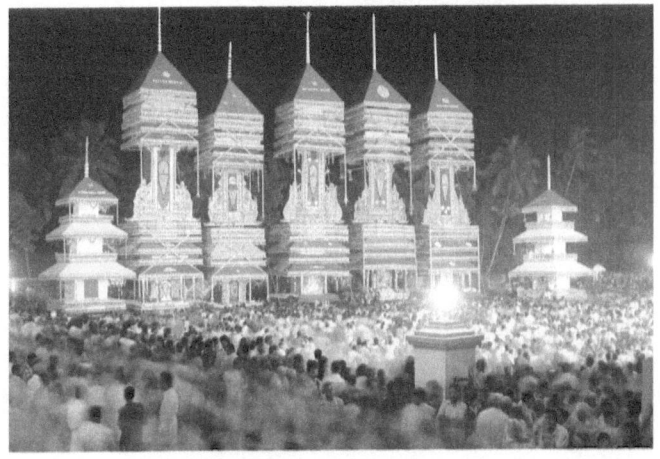

Temporarily built image for Chettikulangara Bharani festival.

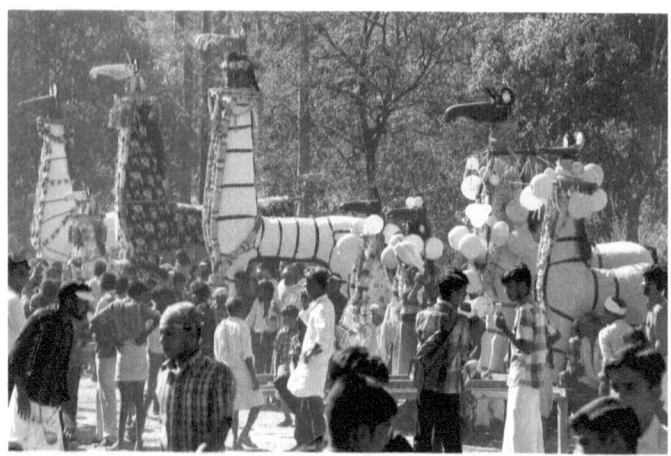

Animal figures for Chinakkathur Pooram- at static stage.

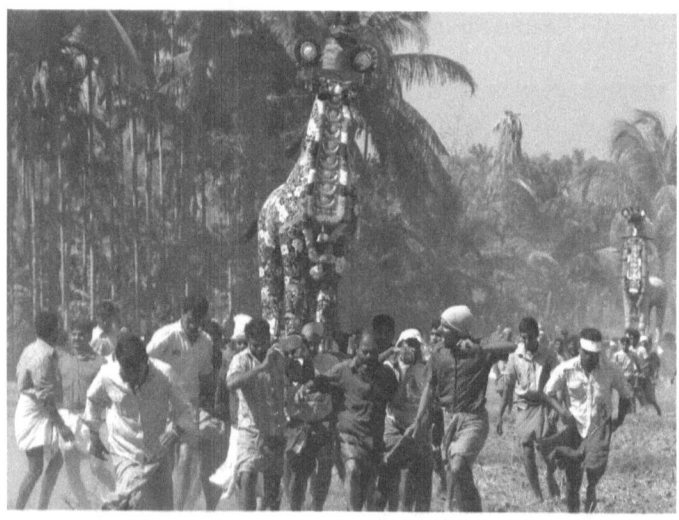

Animal figures on mobility with human force during Machathu Mamangam.

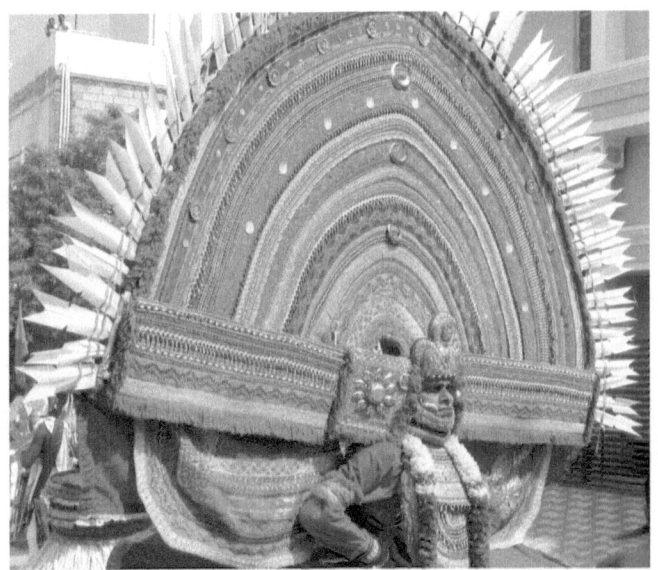

Theyyam image symbolizing Devi with majestic craft work on headgear.

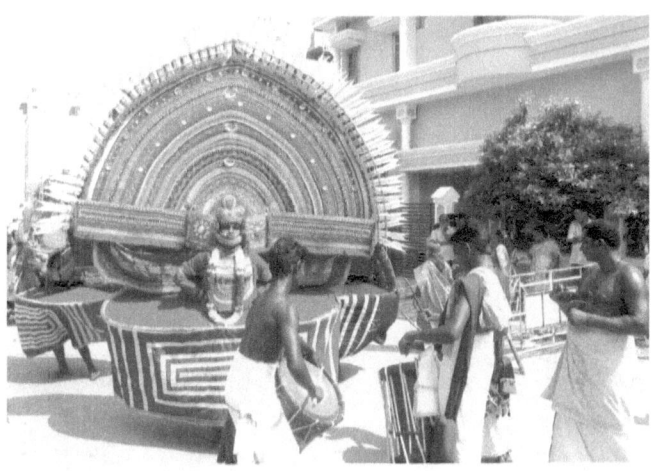

Theyyam performance on a street.

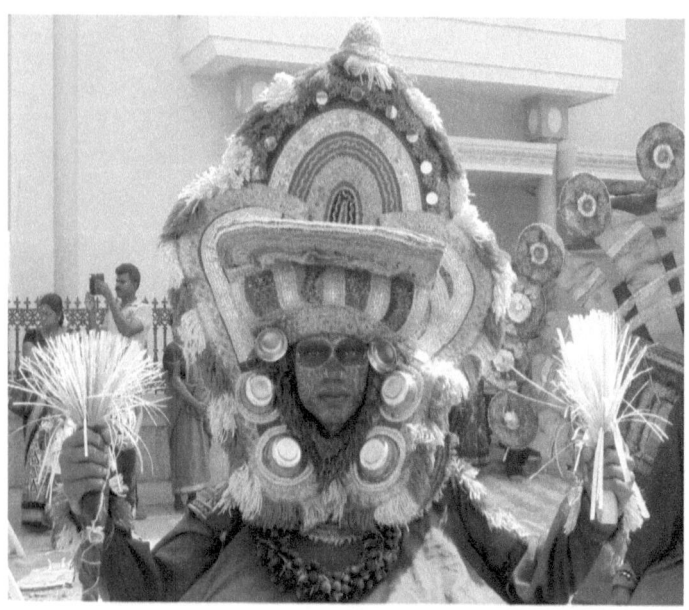

Another image with appealing craft work on it.

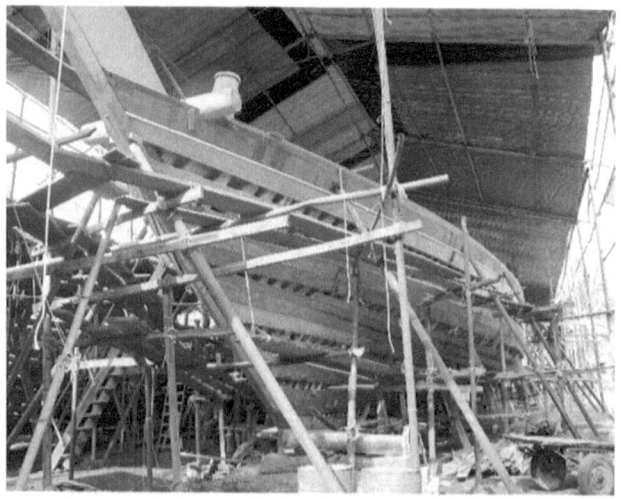

Uru- the ship at delicate fabrication level and craft.

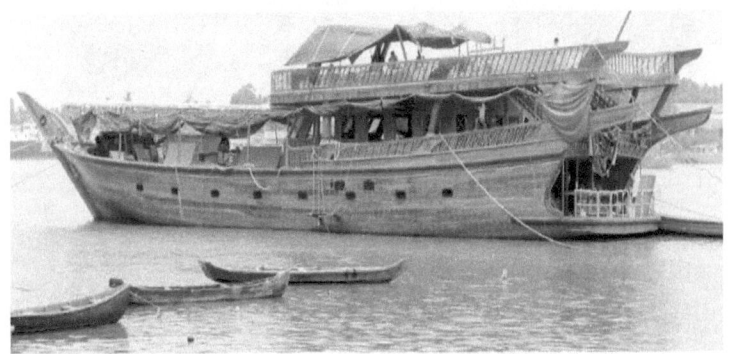

Uru- Ship nearing completion - floating.

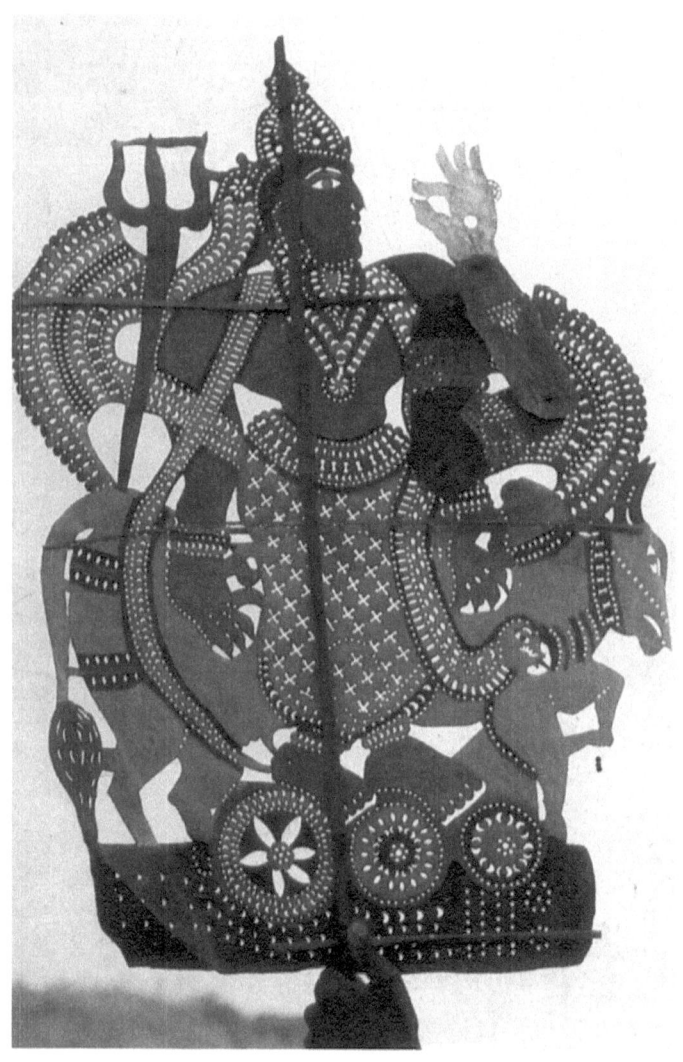

Image of pavakkoothu, Lord Siva.

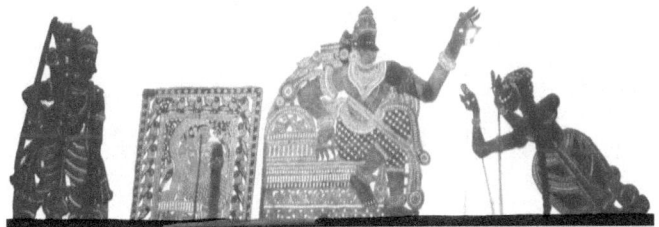

Principal images of Ramayana on stage during pavakkoothu performance.

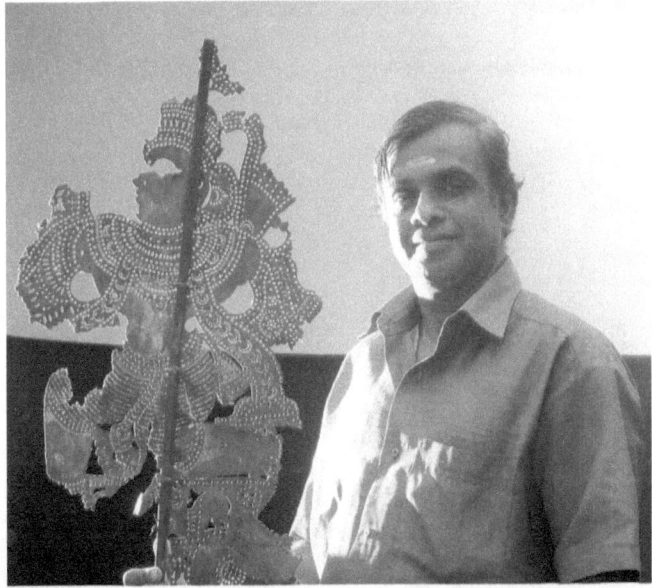

Ramachandra Pulavar, the leading pavakkoothu artist in Kerala.

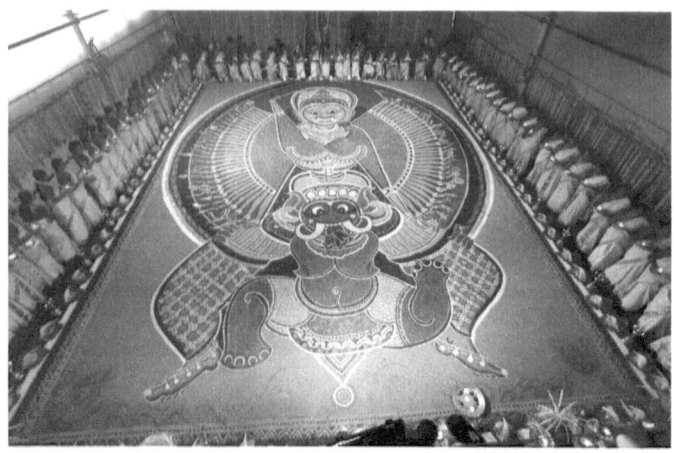

Bhadrakalikalam on worship during Vadakkupurathu Pattu of Vaikkom Mahadeva temple.

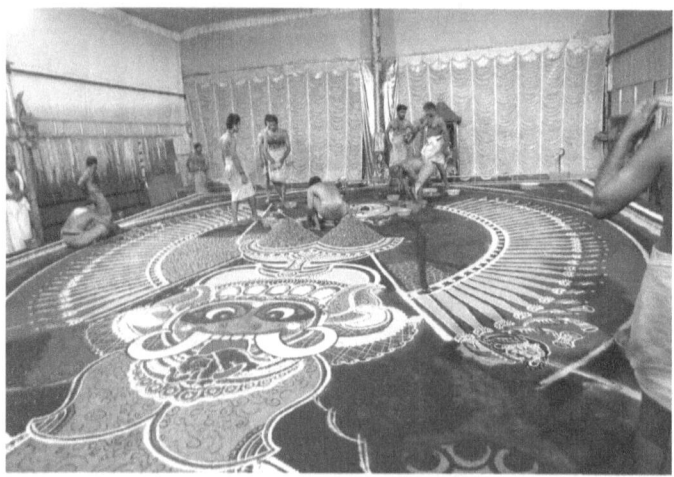

Gopalakrishna Kurup and his disciples at work during Vadakkupurathu Pattu celebrations.

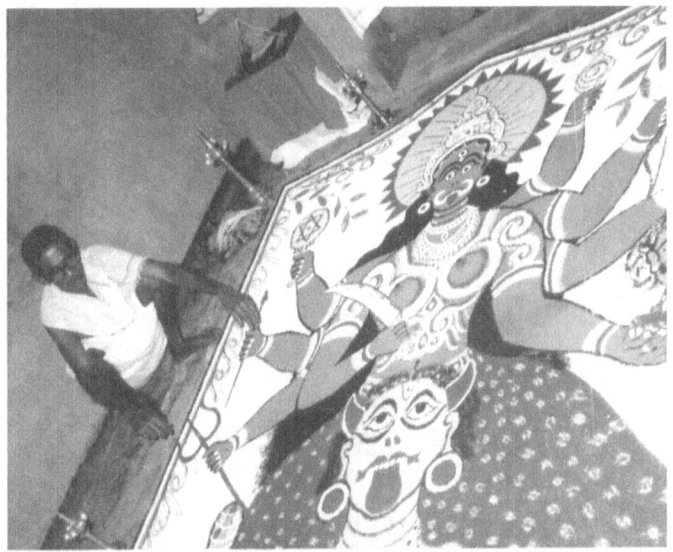

Achutha Paniker, an exponent of Bhadrakalikalam on completion of Devi image.

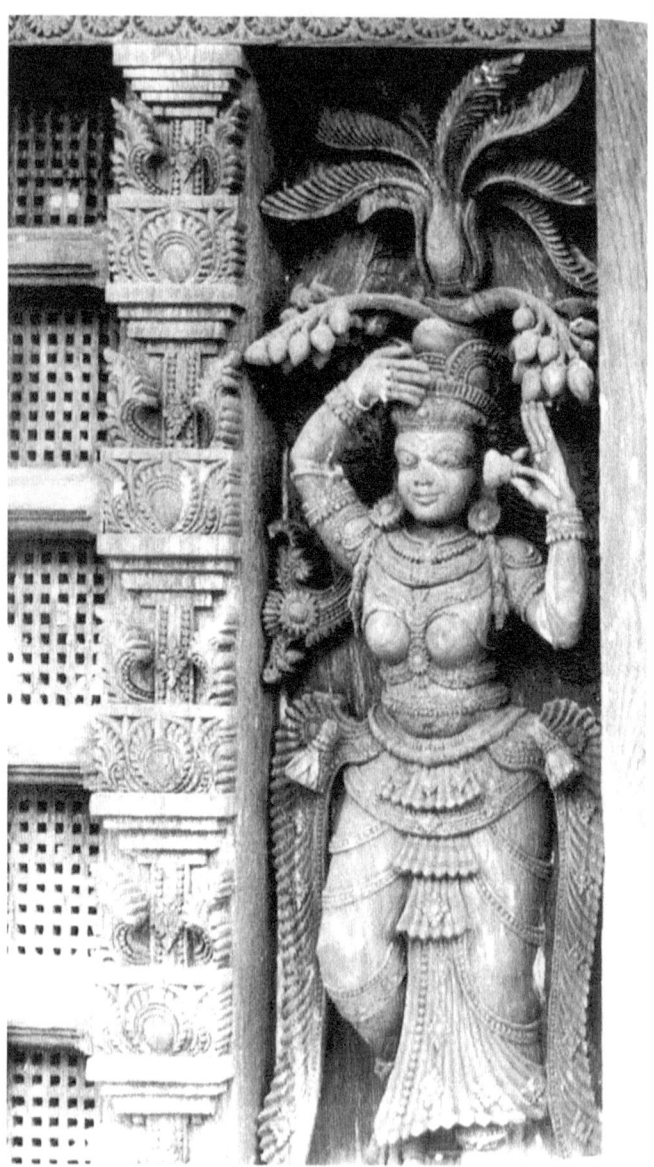

Daru Shilpa of Yakshi image, from Poovappuzha temple.

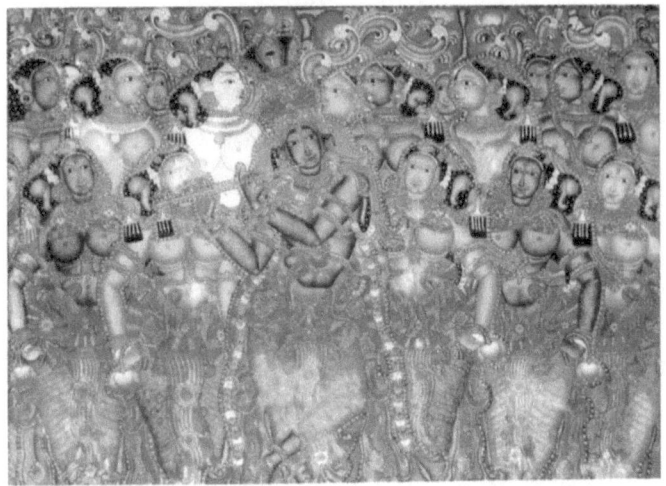

Mural painting at Padmanabhapuram Palace, Sree Krishna and Gopikas.

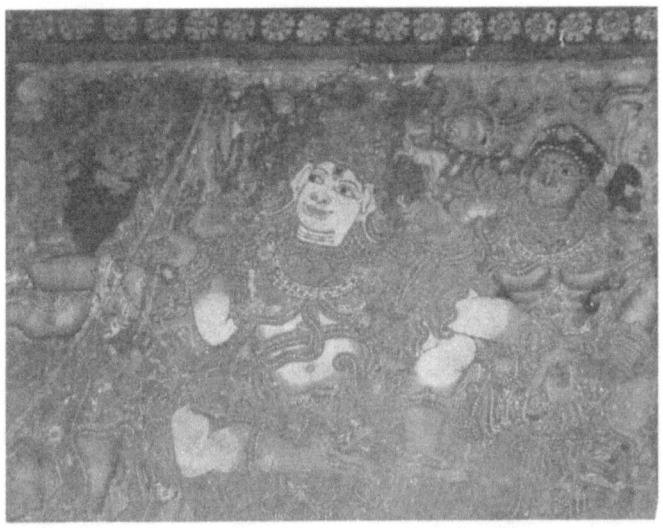

Mural image of Dakshina Murthi at Panayannarkavu Temple.

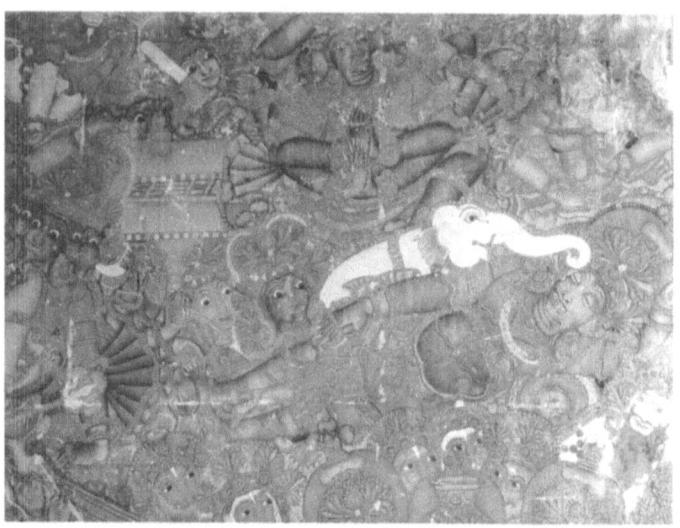

Mural painting- Awaking Kumbhakarna. Mattancheri Palace.

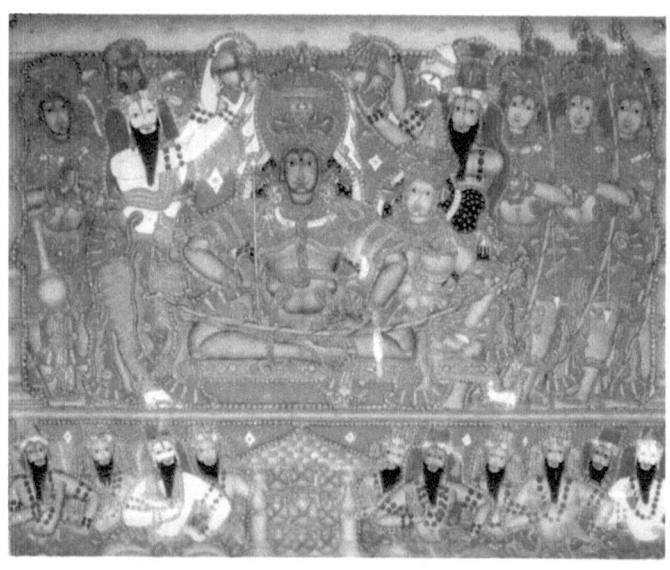

Sree Rama pattabhishekam, Padmanabhapuram Palace.

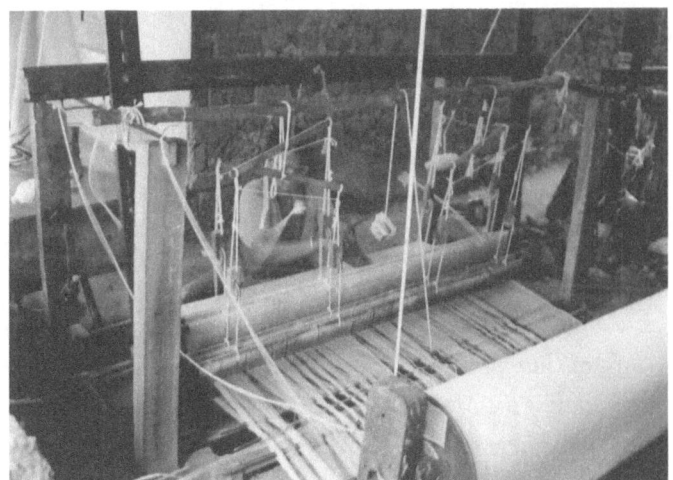

Women working on a pit loom for making cloth.

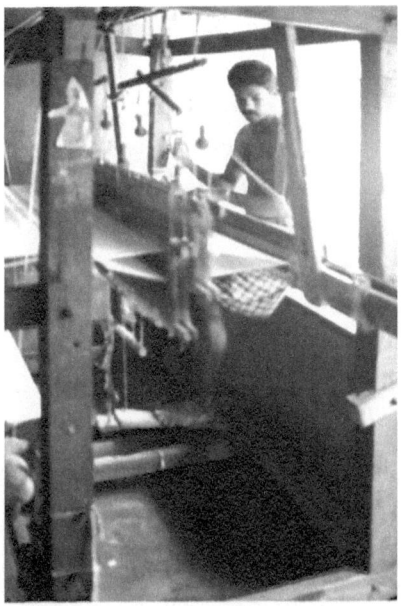

Man working on a stand loom for making cloth.

Notes

1. *Asari. A Malayalam word means the Carpenter and denote a sub caste of Shudras in four caste system.*
2. *Kollan. Malayalam word means the blacksmith.*
3. *Ara. Malayalam word for safe room.*
4. *Padmanabhapuram was once the Capital of Travancore and currently situated in Tamil Nadu, State.*
5. *Attingal is thirty five Kilometers far in the north away from Capital city of Kerala State, Trivandrum.*
6. *Kodali is the Malayalam word for axe.*
7. *Refered here the ancient four caste system with Brahmin, Kshathriya, Vyshya, and Shudra castes in it.*
8. *Uruli, Valkindi, Thalika, and Poothalam are words of Malayalam origin describing various utensils of day to day life and Nilavilakku is the traditional Bronze ceremonial Lamp.*
9. *Attavilakku is made up of bronze in shape of a traditional lamp with enough heights to fall light into the face of actors while Kathakali performances are on.*
10. *Kumbhakar, Kusava, are Malayalam words denotes clay figure makers for terracotta. Kusava is the sub caste of Shudras the fourth category of four caste system.*
11. *Kutta, Vatti, Muram, Parambu, Thadukku are Malayalam words for objectivities utilized in day to day life.*
12. *Chettikulangara is a place in Central Kerala.*
13. *Kuthira: a composed Horse image.*
14. *Puppeteering, Manipulate puppets as in a theatrical performance.*

15. *Pictures are made by using vegetable colors on cow dung pasted floor according to narration in puranic storoes.*
16. *The artists depends up on Dhyana slokas for the iconographic image to be drawn in painting.*
17. *Warrier, Kurup, Marar are belongs to higher castes acknowledged as per the job they are placed in, in temples.*
18. *Balaramapuram is in Trivandrum District where thousands of weavers settled their lives and work in family groups.*

References

Selected Readings and others

1. *Above paper is based on several visits to various localities for personal understandings and communication. Also several people are personally interviewed to follow factual situations.*
2. *"Kerala." Encyclopedia Britannica. Encyclopedia Britannica Online. Encyclopedia Britannica Inc., 2011. Web. 26 December 2011.*
3. *S. Ramachandran Nair, Freedom Struggle in Colonial Kerala, Published in Kalady, 2004. Pages 186.*
4. *Sreedhara Menon, A. Kerala History and its Makers. DC Books.*
5. K N Panikkar, Essays on the History and Society of Kerala, K N Panikkar, Kerala Council for Historical Research.
6. *Vincent A. Smith; A. V. Williams Jackson (30 November 2008). History of India, in Nine Volumes: Vol. II – From the Sixth Century BCE to the Mohammedan Conquest, Including the Invasion of Alexander the Great. Cosimo, Inc. pp. 166*

7. *Pupul Jayakar "The Earthern Drum". IGNCA. 1982. Pages 380.*

8. *Elements of Hindu Iconography by Mr. Gopinath Rao, Page 142*

9. *Folk art of Bengal" by Ajith Mukherjee. Page 221*

10. *K. Krishna Reddy. Indian History. Tata McGraw-Hill Education. Pages. 120*

11. *Udai Prakash Arora; A. K. Singh. Currents in Indian History, Art, and Archaeology. Anamika Publishers & Distributors. pages. 118,*

12. *Nathan Katz (2000). Who Are the Jews of India?. University of California Press. p. 245.*

13. *PN Ravindran (2000). Black Pepper: Piper Nigrum. CRC Press. p. 103.*

14. *K Damodaran in "Indiayude Atmavu" Malayalam Book, Page no 224.*

15. *J. L. Mehta (2005). Advanced Study in the History of Modern India: Volume One: 1707 - 1813. Sterling Publishers Pvt. Ltd. pages.327*

16. *A. Sreedhara Menon (1987). Political History of Modern Kerala. D C Books. Pages- 140.*

17. *Dr. M G Sasi Bhooshan. Keraliya Kala Darsanam, Kerala State Institute of Languages. 2001.*

18. *Dr. M G Sasi Bhooshan. Karalathile Chuvar Chithrangal, Kerala State Institute of Langages. Pages-240.*

19. *Babu Namboodiri K, Our Traditional Leather Shadow Puppeteers. Melinda Books, 2018. Pages. 156.*

Supplementary Elements of Entertainment in Leather Shadow Puppeteering of Andhra Pradesh

Abstract: With stupendous international kindred, leather shadow puppetry is a marvelous folk art form widespread in India. This art form has a role in conception of amusement in all south Indian states, (Kerala, Tamil Nadu, Karnataka and Andhra Pradesh). Apart from its special role on Hindu devotional practices it a well established engagement of entertainment. There are certain families absolutely devoted in puppet making, playing and surviving only with income produced through performances. It is very intricate for provide a normal survival to them because of the strong hostility with other various modern forms of entertainments existing in each corner. However it is the duty of the beholders and beneficiaries to keep the system alive for their continued existence. The certain changes and differences found in puppets and its manipulation in Andhra Pradesh are documented and I have evaluated its relevance here.

Key words: Tholu Bommalatha, Kambaramayanam, Adalpattu, Are, Ranganatha Ramayanam, Ayappudava, Sadya Vazhthal, Puppeteering.

Introduction: From childhood I have been well acquainted with several types of performances conducted in temples offered as worship to deities. This kind of folk associated performances have analogous nature and character which are conducted in temple premises as offering to satisfy the deity for the accomplishment of their wishes and dreams and are related with unforeseen happenings in materialistic life. Habituated reading it was some years ago, I happened to read one of the first books in this area, which was written by K L Krishnankutty Pulavar who was a well-known puppeteer with authentic knowledge in the subject. He was a meticulous performer of Tholpavakoothu, and most likely the first writer of the same in Malayalam the native language. His book "Tolpavakoothu, The Traditional Shadow Puppet Play of Kerala, Vol.-I, Balakandam" was published in 1987.

In 2005, I was invited by Chennai Regional Centre of Lalithakala Akademi, New Delhi to participate in a practicum arranged at Chennai. The puppet manipulating artists from various parts of South India and some contemporary artists including me were invited to participate in the workshop. The idea was to evolve a new technique by exchanging our ideologies with inborn and adapted skills owned by the genuine local village artists. We spent fifteen days and nights, learning, mind storming, discussing, drawing, painting the puppets, cutting the leather, experimenting and recreating the images, scripting, practicing voices, music and mobility chances of each of the images we made. It was amazing for me to watch the way master craft persons from Palghat, Tanjore, Kanyakumari, Bengaluru and Visakhapatinam straightly cut leather with a sharp knife and stitch them to make a huge Ravana horrifying Puppet or smooth colorful pieces joined for a beautiful image of Sita. I have been straightforwardly exposed to performances of shadow puppeteering from all the South Indian states. Among which I found the performance of Andhra based puppetters are keeping some makeable differences from others and its entertainment level is higher than the others when comparing its visual impacts. The differences I have located are the major theme in this essay.

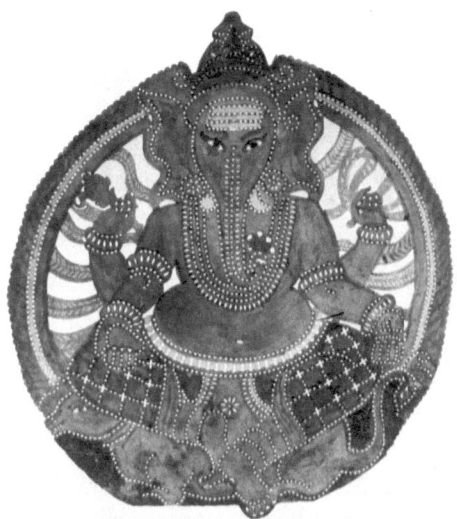

Image of Ganesh, shown at beginning of the puppet play.

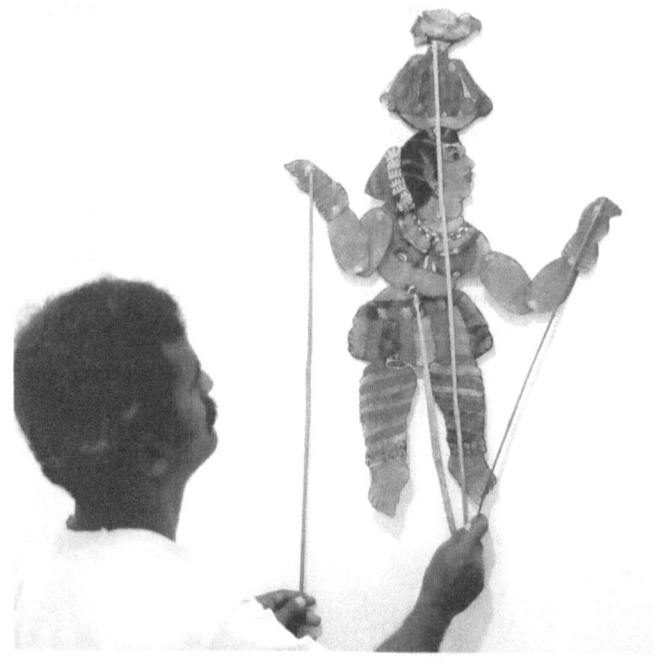

Dancing puppet of Tamil Nadu on manipulation.

General nature of performance: The images according to the story and puranic descriptions are cut from leather made from animals like deer, goat etc without losing its transparency. The images prepared are punched for passage of light as per requirements and colored using limited number of colors prepared naturally[1]. These puppets are strengthened by fixing a bamboo stick at the centre and according to the requirements of movements supposed to be made while performances. Some puppets are made with convenience to move some body portions so the artists can make feeling of a dance performance by a puppet, walking, speaking and even fighting between puppets on the screen.

A screen is made using a big cotton dhoti, and lights made up of broken coconut, oil-cotton thread made lamps are kept behind. The puppets are exposed between the lamps and screen movingly for the colorful shadows to fall on the screen. The artists manipulates the puppets, orate the dialogues narrating the story and sing as per requirements. Also they use accompanying instruments while the story is narrated dramatically in tonal gradations, laughs, cries, shouting, singing, and even running sometimes to place and change puppets according to the requirement of the narration. Most of the times more than one person is involved in entire performance, often all the family members of the artists take part in various actions like controlling lamps, handling puppets, singing, making additional sounds for special effects and in using musical instruments. All happen behind the screen which is invisible for viewers.

Generally the sizes of the puppets are limited under three feat which can be easily handled behind the width and length of the screen made by dhoti. There are differences found in size of puppets, type of leather used, size of screen, number of puppets and puppeteers, accompanying instruments and the ways and manners of presentations from place to place according to the taste of the local people. Generally the stories are taken from Ramayana, but in several occasions they performed different stories as per requirements of the audience. This folk art form is known as Tholpavakoothu in Kerala, Tholu Bommalatha in Andhra Pradesh, Thokala Bommalatha in Karnataka, Ravanaschaya in Orissa and as Chandi Bahulya in Maharashtra[2]. Also this folk art form with variant is popular in Thailand, Malaysia and China.

There are places where contemporary festivals are arranged for puppet play.

Manikya Vasakar in his book "Thiruvachakam" wrote during the growth of Bhakthi cult[3], referred Tholpavakoothu with a sentence "Tholin Pavai koothatai chuzhalvintene"[4]. The text of Thirukural which was written in the first century refers to a kind of street play (Theruvu Natakam)[5]. Also Bharatha describes about a shadow drama in his Natya Sastra[6]. Evidences show the existence of a kind of shadow puppetry during "Wuti" Period in China[7]. It is presumed that the declaration of the existence of shadow puppetry as an enjoyable art form first appeared in Tamil literature. The use of skin for shadow puppetry can be justified with habits of various races by keeping made animal skin on belief of its supernatural power to protect people from evil forces.

There is an existing authentic screen play for Tholpavakoothu in south India. The suggestions for the screen play are based on epic Ramayana as retold by Tamil poet Kambar. There are 12116 stanzas in the Kambaramayanam[8]. The screen play is known as Adalpattu in Tamil Nadu and Kerala. There are 2500 important Stanzas included in the adalpattu of Tholpavakoothu. Even though except some most of these stanzas resemble Kambaramayanam, only few stanzas differ from it in style and content. These variations might have occurred due to the local interference of artists. Ramayanam is the most accepted story with logic of showing it in Devi temples. When Sri Ram went to win war with Ravana and killed him for rescue of Sita, Devi Bhadrakali was busy in carnage of Darikasura, another demon figure in Hindu mythology. As extermination of demons are favorable to heavenly forces like Bhadrakali, the incident of killing Demon Ravana is visually symbolized in another occasion to delight her.

In Kerala, Tamilnadu and Karnataka the traditional puppet manipulators are accustomed with steps followed through centuries in performance. The tholpavakoothu is performed in Devi temples and Siva temples having separate places of worship for Devi. There are more than 120 venues in Kerala where Tholpavakoothu is performed during festivals. Some of the venues have a separate stage permanently built (Koothumadom) and retained for the performances year after year. The performers with help of devotees make temporary stages where permanent facility is absent. The performance based on Kambaramayanam has 21 parts and it takes 21 days of play to complete all. The Adal Pattu is a mixed form of prose and poetry and poetry is sung by participants called 'Koothukavikal'.

The performer begin his speech with following introduction: "by watching the beautiful dance of peacock, hen in the forest tries to imitate the peacock. Just like that our efforts may not be fruitful. We request our wise spectators to forgive the shortcomings and mistakes we may commit during the performance[9]." After introduction the narrator explains specialties of the portion which is proposed to play that day and each character is displayed on the screen. It is followed by Sadyavazhthal meant by 'appraising the feast', during which they elaborately thank everyone who supported them to materialize the play there. The performers are offered with money, fruits and special food items by the devotees during the play. Also special praying with any one of the devotional image is performed during the play in with alternate words other than original adalpattu and it is not considered as mistake or strange as it is expected. According to Kambaramayanam the screen play of the 20th day includes beheading of Ravana. The screen called Azhapudava is removed, washed and dried for the usage of performance on 21st day to eliminate impurities of blood shedding and killing of Ravana, for performing the enthronement of Sree Rama who is the winner. 21st day the stage manager called Madapulavar take out the screen on completion of the play, cut it into pieces and distribute among the devotees to keep in home to deflect all evil forces and curses.

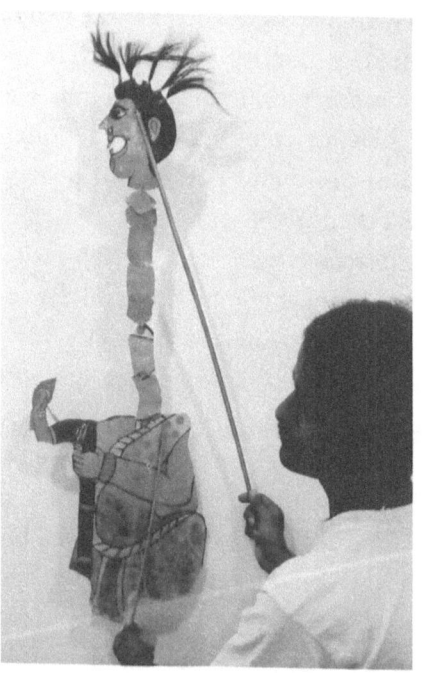

A comedy puppet of Tamil Nadu on manipulation.

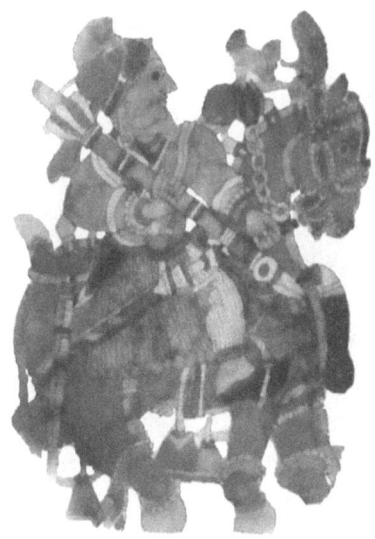

Horse rider. A Centuries old puppet in collection of Artist Kale,
Andhra Pradesh.

Differences in Puppets of Andhra Pradesh

There are serious differences between the images of shadow puppteering in Andhra Pradesh and other places in South India. The family of an artist named Mr. Kale has been engaged in making designs for leather puppets for past many centuries. The seasoned leather is purchased from local market, suitable pictures for puppet shows drawn following puranic traditional job accepted for their family. They stories, finish them with generally accepted iconographic details and appealing colors. They consider it as a devotional duty and sell them to the puppeteers as per their requirements. Mr. Kale lives in Andhra Pradesh and there are some centuries old sample puppets in his care. None of them measure more than three feet height and adequate breadth.

Some of the performers from Andhra Pradesh to whom I was directly exposed were using approximate life size images up to six feet height during performances. Also they manipulated the images to fall shadows in an adequately sized curtain instead of a dhoti. These performers are from genuine puppeteering families and brought up in peculiar cultural backgrounds. Of course the visual range of puppets and aesthetics is high in their productions. The feeling created by the shadows fell on big screen than a dhoti which gather more involvement of spectators. They seem more attractive and influential to anybody watching them. The generated involvement is more passionate, influential and seductive to any viewer.

In personal enquiry I understood that they began to use bigger images since childhood along with smaller ones. Slowly understanding the impact on viewers, they renewed the size though and received more appreciation. Smaller puppets are made to show when object is shown as from far distance. During some occasions like the situations when the growth of Hanuman is to be shown, differently sized images one by one are shown, from small to larger. Except such they usually use puppets made in larger sizes, while the puppeteers in other places in Tamil Nadu, Kerala and Karnataka are using the images in older format, less than 3 feet height. Requirement of larger screen and more efforts are some disadvantages for them. Player will not be able to manipulate a six feet high puppet by sitting. It requires for them to stand behind the screen and in some rare occasions, and it requires more than one person to control and manipulate a single puppet. When such situation comes with more than one or two puppets on screen, it requires two or more people to manipulate and the difficulty of the same is transparent....

Another difference I found in images of Andhra is exceptional mobile nature. The puppets they made for women like Sita, the heroine of Ramayana is made with moving hands, moving legs, moving hips, sometimes even with moving fingers and lips. The heads of certain images and the lips, they are made with more mobility. These are advantages for the meticulous puppet manipulators. Performing with mobility increased puppet is difficult but they are able to manipulate them more freely even to show minutest details of a movement. So that the performer will be able to make replica of the movements of a dancer, performer, and deliberate war phases more accurately. All these possibilities are advantageous for attracting more people and acquire demand for their program. The elements added are confirmed to make more entertainment for its viewers.

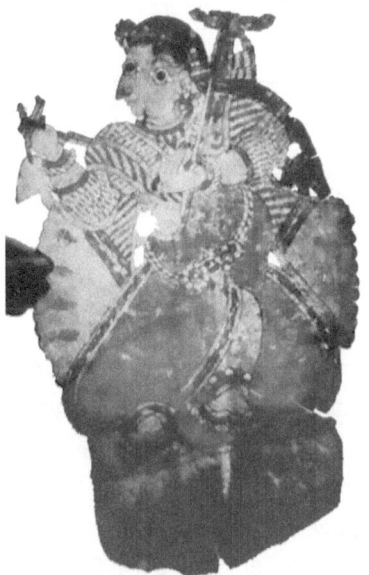

Horse rider. Centuries old puppet in collection of Artist Kale. Andhra Pradesh.

The third and most major diversity is the difference of the story they uses in Andhra for puppeteering. The essence of story is tailored from Ramayana, like Kambaramayanam is the base of story in Karnataka, Kerala and Tamil Nadu. But the major source of Andhra Pradesh is Ranganatha Ramayanam wrote by Gona Budha Reddy[10]. The artist uses the same lyrics used in Yakshaganam, another well known folk performance of Andhra Pradesh for Shadow Puppeteering. The theatricality of Yakshaganam is higher than any other folk art, performance of Andhra Pradesh. The performance and body movements in Yakshaganam are higher influential than other such forms. The puppeteers always tries to replicate human movement in their puppets and the viewers get a more live theatrical situation by use of similar movements of Yakshaganam in Puppet manipulation. Which makes attraction to art form much higher than during the usual use of small images for Kambaramayanam. The viewers in all venues, in Andhra Pradesh and other places of South India are getting entirely different results of Rasa[11], which reach superior in the viewers of Andhra. When considering the theatrical impact on audience through puppeteering with larger images, the stories Indrajith vadham, Keechaka vadham, Veera Abhimanue, and Padmavyuham are with high impact on viewers of Andhra Pradesh.

My direct contact with the artists made opportunities to communicate with them elaborately. They agreed that they have to adjust their life and lifestyles for the continuation of their practice. Always they try to modulate their performance in a manner they could satisfy their appreciators. They practiced their life in which they never argued for benefits. They were satisfied with what offered to them each day after practice of their performance which is very low according to the labor they produce. Further studies on the origin of puppeteers in Andhra led me to the fact that the early puppeteers were shifted from Maharashtra some centuries ago to Andhra and followed the basic wandering life that depends up on the availability of work. A number of families in this clan are available near the border villages of Bellari and Hindpur. They increased the sizes of the images slowly to bring better impact on viewers and replaced the story narration in a more appealing manner successfully.

Conclusion: The puppeteers of Andhra, Karnataka, Tamil Nadu, and Kerala were Nomads. The first settled among them were the families in Kerala which was at least one and a half century ago. The people in this clan are known as Pulavar and enjoying normal lives with a social status. The puppeteers of Kerala say a story of Chinna Thampi[12] about the first Pupeteer in Kerala but which has no solid evidences. Considering other symptoms of practice it is safe to consider their chance of settling earlier in Kerala and finding social support for their long stay here. The puppeteers of other states directly agree and accustomed with their state of survival. They all had a past of travel from one place to other along with everything they acquired during life along with other members of the family until find a new venue suitable for survival.

The puppet manipulators in Karnataka and Tamil Nadu are still living their vegetarian lives on road sides in which they are not bothered much. They are worried about their food, survival and puppeteering and further possibilities of it. The puppeteers speak "Ara" a dialect of Marathi within their family and hold a vegetarian life. "Mutharamma"[13] a form of Devi is their major Goddess.

As time passes the light source was changed to petro-maxes. In the forties the new source of electric light became popular. Now all people except in the Hindu devotional venues uses electric lights for the performance. They are more powerful and the efficiency to penetrate through the leather which is several times bigger than beam of oil lamps. All the puppeteers perform in traditional format, but the puppeteers of Tamil Nadu are more innovative in their approach and found various themes to perform stories about rain water collection (Mazhaineersamipoo), the importance of growing trees (MaramValirpoo), cleanliness (Sukhacharam), elimination of AIDS, Elimination of Polio etc. They adjust the play for advanced viewers, arranges programs for performance suitable for modern life, the satirical stories self made, and newly shaped puppets with them. It is necessary for them to search for viewers near large factories, where the ordinary and humble people gather, in schools etc. There are several stories kept by them to entertain the adolescent viewers.

Garalattom, Kavadiyattom, Vaymoodarathu, Kadasaranam, Peyattom, Swamiyattom are some of them, to which people crowded. The performer and artist Muthu Lakshmana Rao made new stories following independence struggles and various political issues, Dandhi March, Jalianwala-bagh etc. To attract large audiences they made a large number of puppets- various political leaders, Gandhi, Kastruba Gandhi, Nehru etc. – according to the requirements.

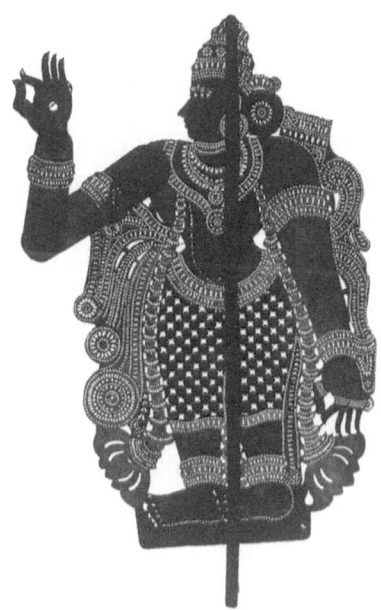

Sree Rama on move, a Kerala puppet with high decorations.

As an effort to reduce cost of entire production and to save money, they started avoiding leather and began to use plastic sheets, polythene, cloth, and even thick paper for the creation of puppets using chemical oxide colors on it. Also color slides, color masks and fluorescent lights are used to make the performance more attractive. But the puppeteers in Kerala and Andhra are still following the traditional set up and perform ceremonially at least occasionally in devotional atmospheres. Generally the puppet makers of Kerala and Andhra draw the pictures on leather themselves. But at least some of them approach local traditional artists for beautiful designs and drawings. The designs of puppets are different from each other and in Kerala; the puppets resemble the images drawn in mural paintings due to involvement of traditional painters in them. Considering dependence on light source to create shadows falling in screen, coordinated sounds and music, narrative qualities, the play of leather puppets may be considered as the older format of today's massive entertainment, the feature film. But with the modern invention of lens shadow images that fall on them can be made into several times bigger. It took prime attention of viewers with its mobile nature and ability to create exact sounds according to the requirements of the projected shadows. But the society did not put into practice to wipe out any such substantial existence of local folk art forms. By adapting affinities towards devotional and ideological human needs, the puppeteers continue their efforts to interact to the mass within their limitations.

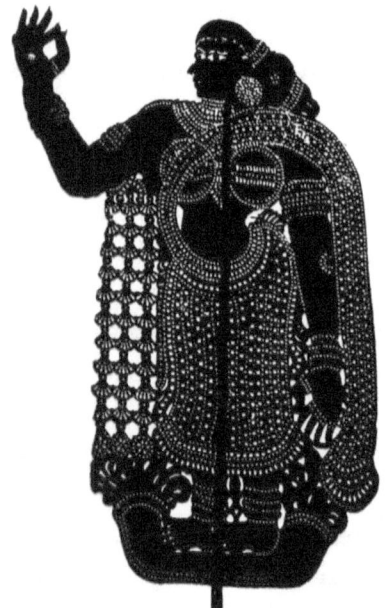

Sita, highly decorated image with motifs of Kerala Mural painting.

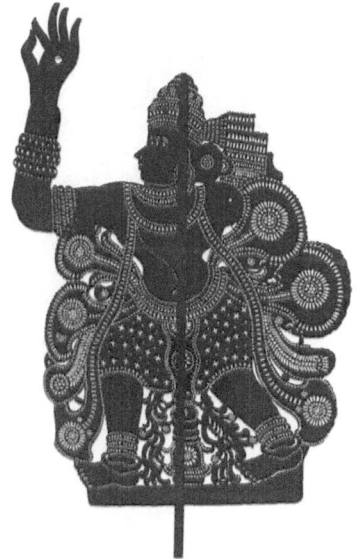

Lakshmana on move, a Kerala puppet.

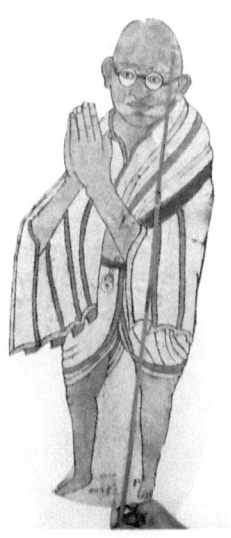

Social element, Gandhi at Dandhi march, Tamil Nadu Puppet.

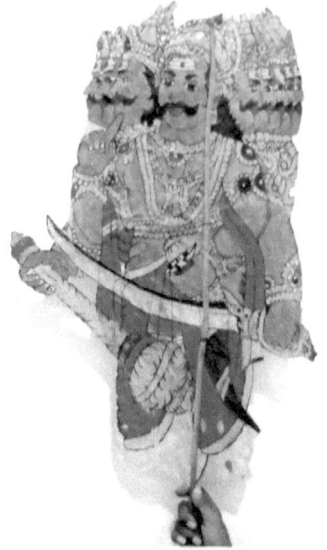

Ravana, Tamil Nadu puppet.

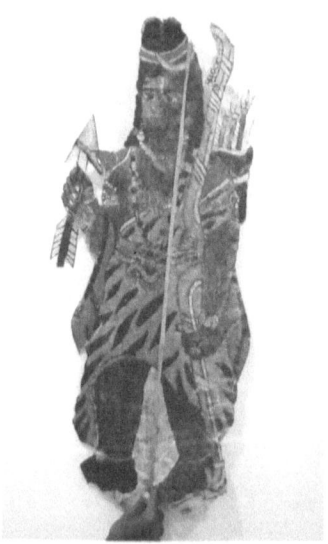

Lord Shiva from Karnataka.

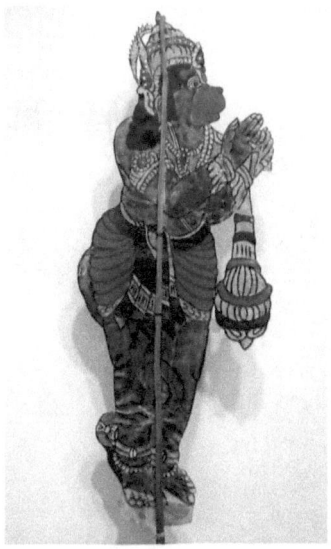

Hanuman, from Karnataka.

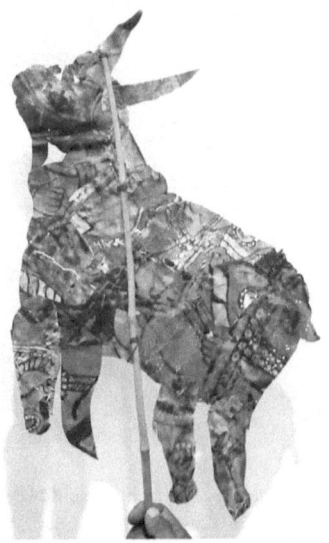

Puppet with use of cloths.

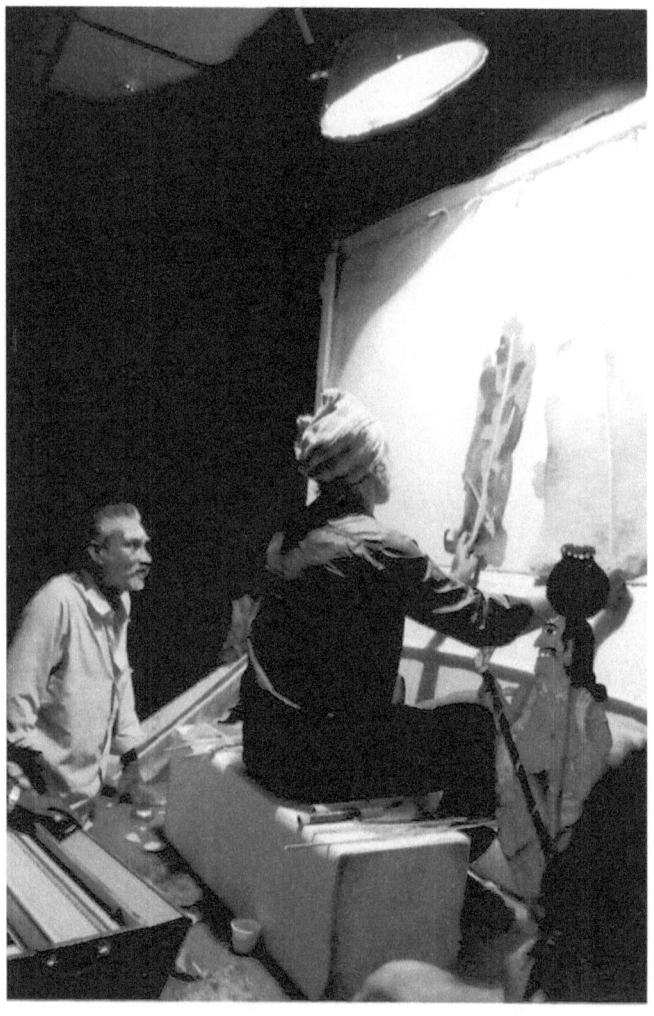

Performance with electric lamp. Tamil Nadu puppets.

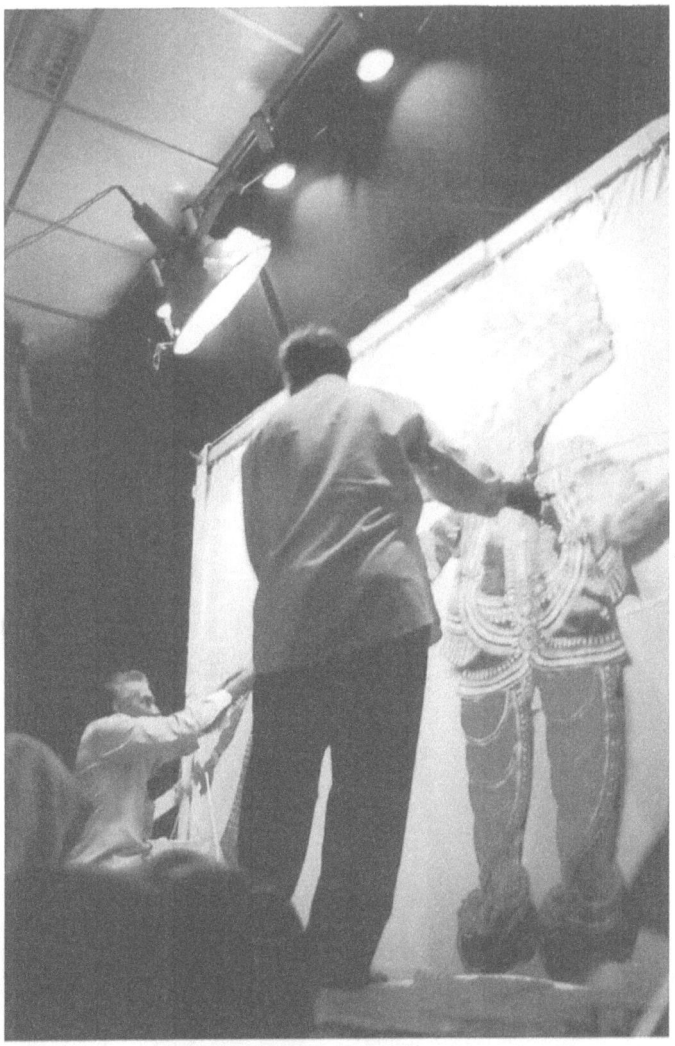

Puppets of Andhra Pradesh presenting with use of electric light by standing behind big screen.

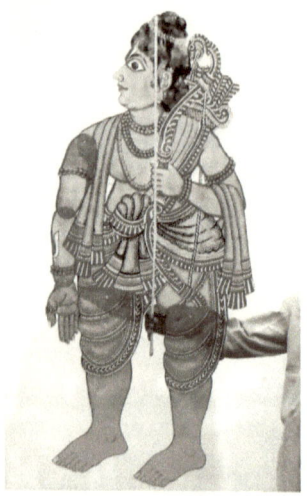

Lakshmana. Andhra Pradesh.

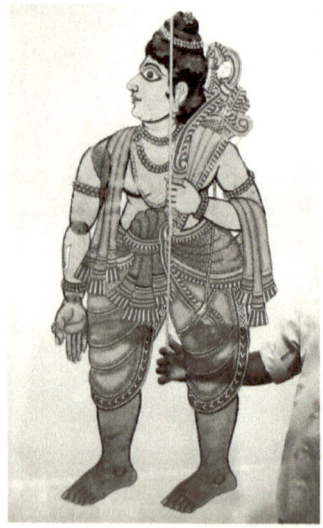

Sree Rama, Andhra Pradesh.

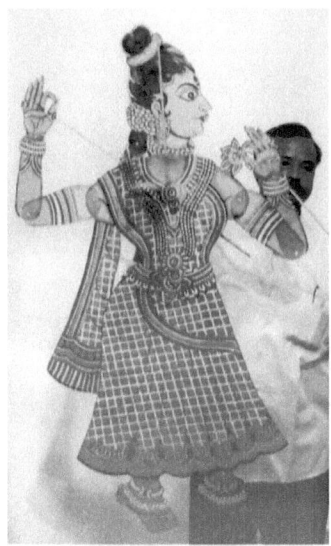

Dancing Sita, Andhra Pradesh.

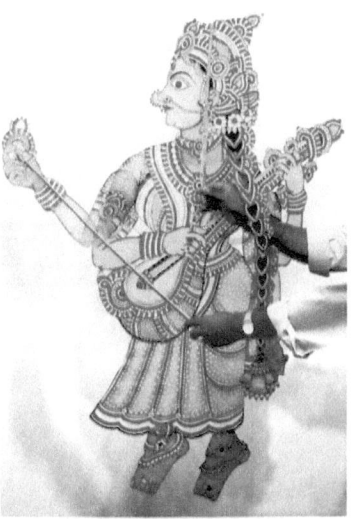

Moving, Saraswati Devi image, Andhra Pradesh.

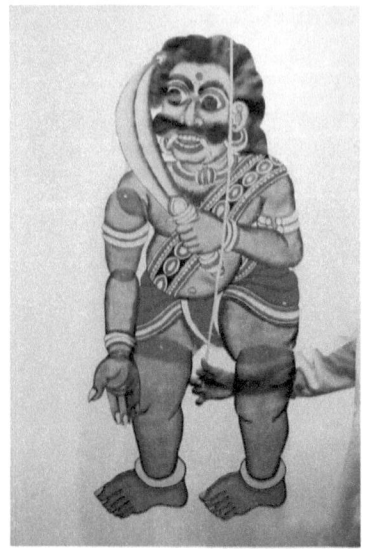

A demon figure, Andhra Pradesh.

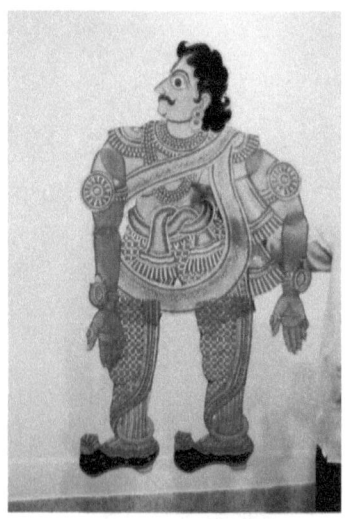

Kubera, Andhra Pradesh

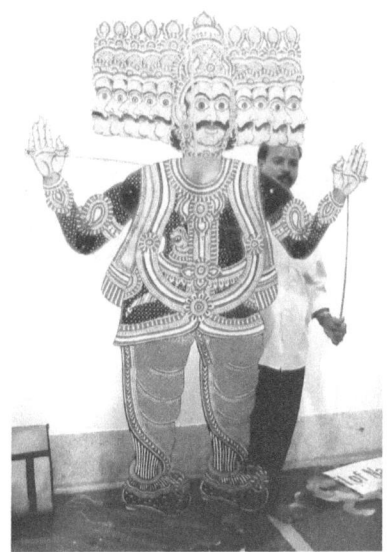

Ravana, Andhra Pradesh.

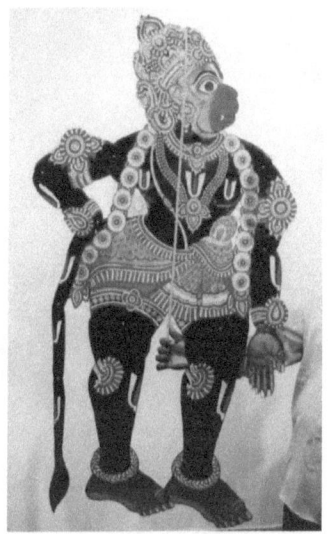

Hanuman, Andhra Pradesh.

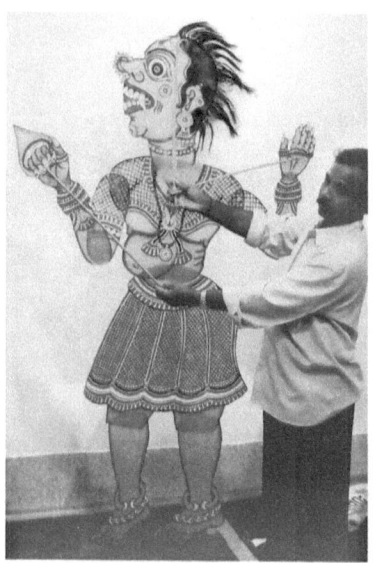

Shurpanakha, Andhra Pradesh.

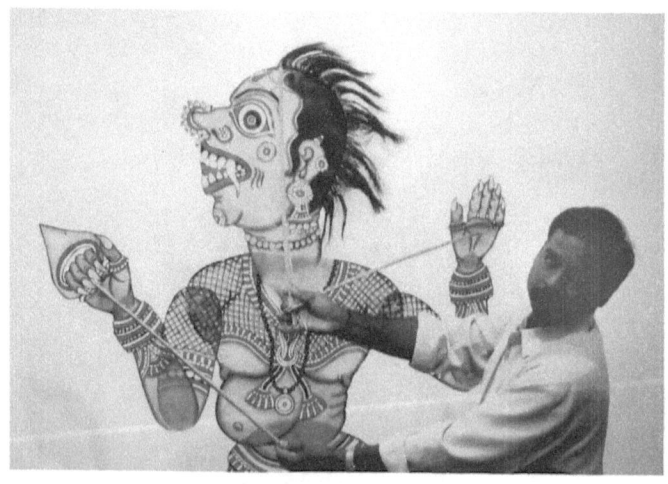

Shurpanakha on manipulation.

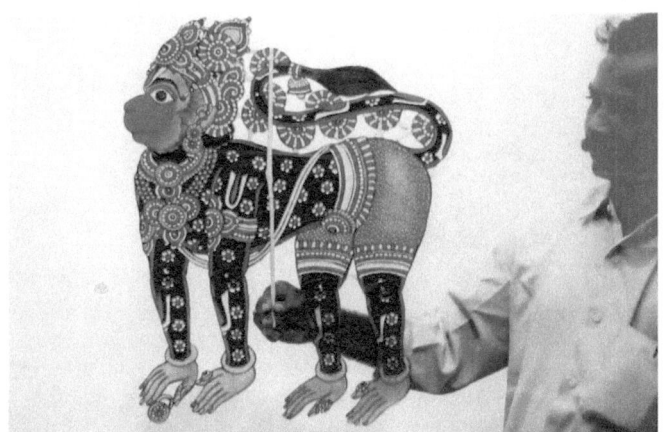

Small Hanuman, Andhra.

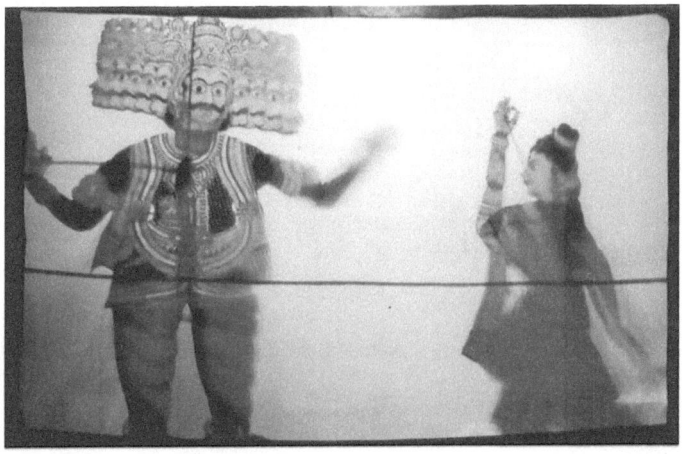

Ravana and Sita on Screen.

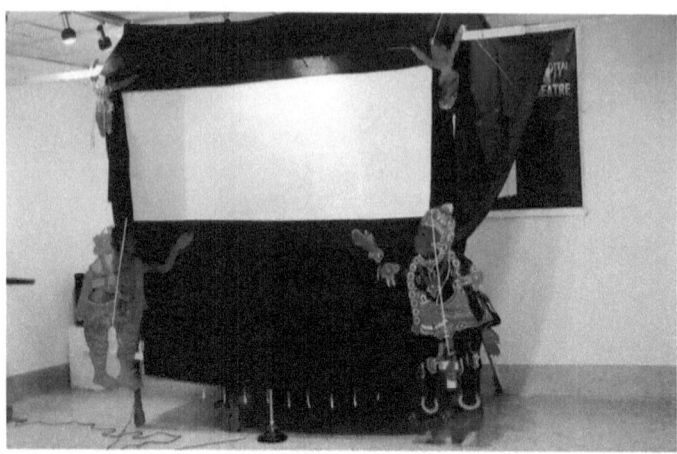

A modern theatre for small puppets.

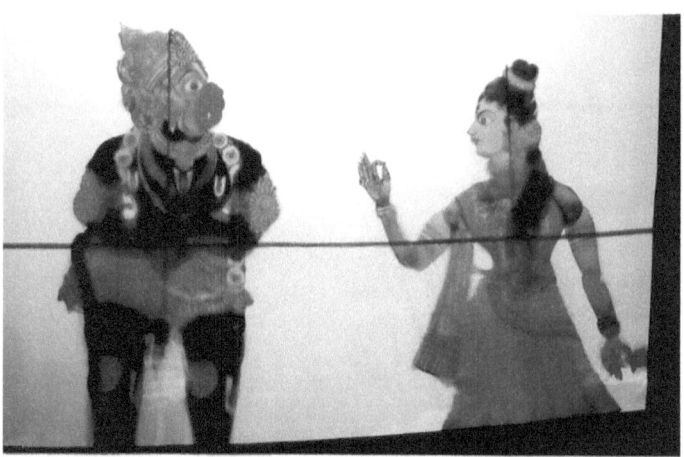

Hanuman and Sita on screen.

Notes

1. *Making colors from natural objects, black from Lamp Black, Red from Kasava tree juice, Green from Amari leaves etc.*

2. *Information bulletin of Nee Enrgee, Shadow theatre festival presented by Kalari foundation, Coimbatore. 2005.*

3. *Bhakthi cult. The Bhakti movement is a Hindu religious movement in which the main spiritual practice is loving devotion among the shivite and Vaishnava saints-originated in Ancient Tamil country. Referencesfrom-http://en.wikipedia.org /wik i/ Bhakti_ movement*

4. *Thiruvachakam- 51 subgroups of poems, is the first writing about his life and his Siva-experience by Manikyavachagar the great Saivite saint. References from (http://www.arunachala-ramana. org/ forum /index. php?topic=271.0)*

5. *Thirukural-Tamil: also known as the Kural-is a classic of couplets or Kurals (1330 rhyming Tamil couplets) or aphorisms celebrated by*

6. *Tamils, authored by Thiruvalluvar, and is the first work focuses on ethics in Dravidian literature.*

7. *NatyaShastra by Bharata. The NatyaShastra by Bharata is the main dramatic theory of the Sanskrit drama which is wrote by sage Bharata. It provides the rules of writing and performing music, dance and theatre and it originally dealt with stage craft.*

8. *Wu-di (also said Wu-Ti) -Period. The Jin Dynasty (pinyinjìn, 265-420) followed the Three Kingdoms and preceded the Southern and Northern Dynasties in China. The dynasty was founded by the Sima family, pinyin*

Sīmă. References from. http://www.knowledgerush.com/ kr/encyclopedia/Chin_Wu-ti/

9. *Kambar- Kambaramayanam -The original version of Ramayana was written by Sage Valmiki. This epic of Kambar describes in 24,000 verses tells of a Raghuvamsa prince, Rama of Ayodhya, whose wife Sita was abducted by Ravana, a mighty emperor*

10. *G Venu. Puppetry and Lesser Known Dance Traditions of Kerala. Published by Natana Kairali in 2004. Also he wrote the introduction to the book wrote by K L Krishnankutty Pulavar titled Tolpavakoothu-The Traditional Shadow Puppet Play of Kerala, in 1987.*

11. *Ranganatha Ramayanam. Is the famous work of Gona Buddha Reddy lived during the 13th century so actually belonged to the Kakatiyaperiod. Reference. http:// en.wikipedia.org/wiki/ Reddy_dynasty #Literature_ During_The_Reddy_Rule*

12. *Rasa is the juice of various elements causes beauty, entertainment and salvation according to Indian Aesthetics.*

13. *Chinna Thampi: Presented Kambarama -yanam in a manner enjoyable to all people irrespective of caste differences when he was not permitted to hear chanting of Ramayana when went to higher caste residence.*

References

1. *K L Krishnankutty Pulavar "Tolpavakoothu -The Traditional Shadow Puppet Play of Kerala." Published by the author. 1987.*

2. *G. Venu. "Puppetry and Lesser Known Dance Traditions of Kerala." Book published by Natana Kairali in 2004.*

3. *Information bulletin of Nee Enrgee, Shadow theatre festival presented by Kalari foundation, Coimbatore. 2005.*
4. *Babu Namboodiri K "Our Traditional Leather Shadow Puppeteers, Leather Shadow Puppeteers in South India." Melinda books, Pages 158. 2018.*

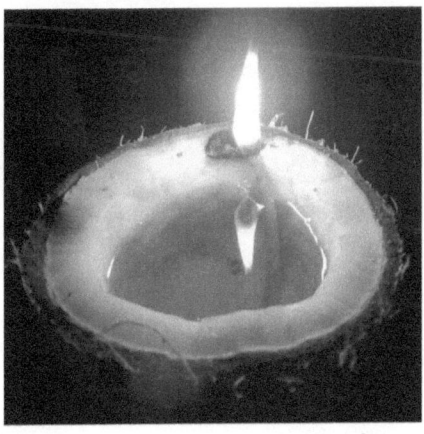

Coconut Brocken and made a lamp out of it.

Images Courtesy: Common files of images widely available are utilized otherwise are noted where ever they are.

About the Author

Babu Namboodiri K

Babu Namboodiri K born in 1964, completed BFA Painting from College of fine Arts, Trivandrum, in 1987. He continued studies at College of Art New Delhi till 1990 and completed MFA in painting with Silver medal for best painting. After a short period of teaching art he joined National Museum Institute, New Delhi for research studies under the well known author and Humanist Mulk Raj Anand. In 1998, he was awarded the most known Japanese Govt. fellowship the Mombusho and was a research fellow at Tokyo National University of Fine Arts till 2000.

Babu Namboodiri K represented India in more than twenty International Exhibitions including Asian Art Biennale at Dhaka- Bangladesh 1993, Triennale India New Delhi- India 1994, Artsits communication program and residency at Yamana Shi-Ken, Japan 1999, Asian artist;'s exhibition at Yoshi foundation, Tokyo, Japan 2000, International Exhibition at Gudalupe, Mexico 2005, Print Art Biennale Exlibris, Mexico 2005, 1st Romanian

Biennale 2005, First International exhibition of Male-Maldives Administration 2005, 10th Triennale India Camp and Exhibition at Bangalore-India 2007 and Bharat Bhawan Print Art Biennale, Bhopal-India 2010 and in quite a number of exhibitions. He has Participated in more than 150 Exhibitions including National/All India Art Exhibitions and others, and held 20 Individual Exhibitions in most important Art Galleries in India, also held in Tokyo 1999 and Busan-Korea 2002.

Participated in many Artist Camps and Residencies, he attended international residency programs in Japan, Maldives Administration, Bangalore India and Budapest-Hungary. He has visited countries Japan, Singapore, Maldives Administration, Hungary, Germany, France, Poland, Czech Republic, Italy, Slovakia and Austria with art and related programs.

Recipient of various awards and recognitions - Kerala Lalitha Kala Academy in 1986 and 87, Silver medal from College of Art, New Delhi 1989, All India Fine Arts and Crafts Society New Delhi purchase award 2004, UGC research fellowships from 1991-1997, The International research fellowship from Mombusho, Japan. Paintings of Babu Namboodir K are in various acquisitions in various countries in the world.

Written a number of research papers and articles in both Malayalam and English, published in research Journals and popular magazines, received research fellowship from University grants commission and International research fellowship from Mombusho, Japan, Babu Namboodiri K wrote and published his first book on Shadow puppeteering in South India in 2018. This is his second book in English.

Babu Namboodiri K, lives in the city of Trivandrum with his spouse Mrs. Roopa D Potti and daughters Lekshmipriya B and Vishnupriya B.

Contact: babunamboodiri@yahoo.com